What Peop

Fairy Herb

Fairy Herbs for Fairy Magic – A Practical Guide to Fairy Herbalism blends folklore, experience, and magic into a cohesive whole, centered on fairies. Perfect for witches following a fairy-led path or anyone who is curious about the intersection of fairies and herbs, this book is both a practical guide and an invitation for the reader to seek their own connection.
Morgan Daimler, author of *Fairycraft* and *Travelling the Fairy Path*

Fairy Herbs for Fairy Magic is a practical book on herb and fairy lore, and how the two intersect. Daniela Simina is a lifelong practitioner of traditional Romanian fairy magic as well as having a solid research background in Irish fairy lore. She also really knows about herbs and their magical uses. The book starts with an examination of the fairy faith, fairy magic, and partnerships between humans and fairies in history and folklore. This sets the groundwork for chapters covering how herbs can be used both for interactions with fairies and in spells to cleanse, protect, heal, attract love and promote general wellbeing. This book offers a wealth of information and would be a wonderful reference work for any witch's shelf.
Lucya Starza, author of *Poppets and Magical Dolls, Scrying,* and *Rounding the Wheel of the Year*

In this book you are invited into a unique exploration of the world of Fairy and their associated herbs. Simina covers lore from Romania, Ireland and Norse sources in a thoughtful yet highly instructive manner. A thorough mix of scholarship and personal gnosis, this book takes you on a journey of enchantment and wisdom. If you have even a passing interest in herblore and fairy, you will not be disappointed in this captivating book. *Fairy Herbs for Fairy Magic* by Daniela Simina truly delivers to both the novice and those well versed on the subject. To those that wish to reach out to Fairy and learn of their associated herbs there is no better place to begin.

Ryan McClain, author of *Abnoba: Celtic Goddess of the Wilds* and *Frigg: Beloved Queen of Asgard*

If I had a dedicated Fairy Library, I would make sure it includes *Fairy Herbs for Fairy Magic*. Daniela gifts fairy seekers with a special practical guide on how plants and fairies work together. *Fairy Herbs for Fairy Magic* is a great aid for researchers by providing enough references for a deeper dive - if that is what you wish. But not only is the book informative, it also offers plenty of opportunities to learn through practice. *Fairy Herbs for Fairy Magic* is an enjoyable read too, which makes it all the more an offering to the fairy people out there. This is one book that all those interested in fairies should add to their collection of fairy lore. A must have!

Ness Bosch, author of *Magic Bones, Sacred Bones*

Pagan Portals

Fairy Herbs for Fairy Magic

A Practical Guide to Fairy Herbal Magic

Pagan Portals

Fairy Herbs for Fairy Magic

A Practical Guide to Fairy Herbal Magic

Daniela Simina

MOON
BOOKS

London, UK
Washington, DC, USA

CollectiveInk

First published by Moon Books, 2024
Moon Books is an imprint of Collective Ink Ltd.,
Unit 11, Shepperton House, 89 Shepperton Road, London, N1 3DF
office@collectiveinkbooks.com
www.collectiveinkbooks.com
www.moon-books.net

For distributor details and how to order please visit the 'Ordering' section on our website.

Text copyright: Daniela Simina 2023

ISBN: 978 1 80341 548 2
978 1 80341 556 7 (ebook)
Library of Congress Control Number: 2023936081

A CIP catalogue record for this book is available from the British Library.

Design: Lapiz Digital Services

UK: Printed and bound by CPI Group (UK) Ltd, Croydon, CR0 4YY
Printed in North America by CPI GPS partners

We operate a distinctive and ethical publishing philosophy in all areas of our business, from our global network of authors to production and worldwide distribution.

Contents

Also by Daniela Simina

Where Fairies Meet
Parallels between Irish and Romanian Fairy Traditions
ISBN 978 1 80341 09 7

A Fairy Path
The Memoir of a Young Fairy Seer in Training
ISBN 978 1 80341 402 7

Anychair Yoga
IBSN-13: 978 1 46815 094 0

To the Ælfe.
Special thanks to Cat for throwing me into the deep end:
it was the fastest way to learn to swim in elven waters.

Foreword

Morgan Daimler

Beul eidhin agus croidhe cuilinn
(A mouth of ivy and a heart of holly)
Irish proverb

The subject of fairies and plants is hardly a new one, being a topic that has been discussed across literature and folk belief for many years, but it is a deceptive topic, a subject that seems simple on the surface but which is complicated and nuanced in unexpected ways. When we dig below that simple-seeming surface we find plants that draw fairies and which repel them, plants that seem to belong to them, and plants which they – in various guises and through various means – have taught humans to use. We find a deep history of witches and magic workers who were connected to fairies and whose relationships involved or included plants. We find plants that were used to ward fairies off and plants that invited them in, which broke their enchantments or which represented their presence in a place. When we dig, we find that the folklore of fairies and the modern practices associated with fairies is full of herbs, trees, resins, and recipes. But not, perhaps, in the ways many people will expect.

When the subject of fairies and plants arises it is often discussed through a very strong, very modern lens which, leaning heavily on theosophy, sees fairies' connections to the natural world as a subservient one and as an enlivening one. That is, fairies are reduced to the power that serves the natural world and allows plants to flourish, narrowing and limiting who and what they are, as well as often softening them into something more palatable. Discussion of the subject – and books about it – also tend to lean too heavily into the author's opinions and personal gnosis. All of this can have a certain value but also presents a distorted view that creates and feeds on itself, leaving those curious about the subject with little to draw on unless they research it all themselves, and that is a difficult proposition.

Fairy Herbs for Fairy Magic is not that kind of book. What you are about to read is a blend of older beliefs and newer ideas, tempered through research and personal experience. This isn't the 'flower fairies' of Cicely Mary Barker but rather herbs and trees associated with fairies across folklore and modern practice, a weaving together of myth and belief into a practical modern guide. Fairies are powerful mercurial beings and Daniela Simina's work here shows them in all their complexity, both benevolent and dangerous, while offering a roadmap for readers to follow in engaging with them and with the plants connected to them. This is a book which will teach you about more than just fairies and about more than just plants; it will teach you about the power to be found in connecting to fairy teachings and belief through the living earth. Magic is a co-creative process, and this book invites you to learn how to participate in that process in an engaged and respectful way.

Walk through a grove of apple trees, appreciating the symbolism that lies within every branch and fruit. Respect the sanctity of a lone hawthorn on a hill. Learn of the power that exists in Rose and the defensive uses of Mugwort across cultures. Find the beauty in something as simple as water, and see how it works with everything else. Connect to fairies with and through plants and grow a deeper understanding of both as they intersect with your magic.

Fairies are beings who are intertwined with the human world, but foreign to it, who are connected to certain plants and trees not as spirits of those things but as spirits with knowledge of the power of those things who are willing to pass that knowledge on to humans. They are beings who can make use of these growing things themselves and who may feel a certain possessiveness about some of them. In short the relationship between fairies and herbs and trees is complex and many layered one, but one which humans who are willing to pay attention to their lessons can learn about and learn from. What follows is a guide to doing just that, leading you deeper into practices that focus on fairies through the intermediary of plants and of water, of wisdom and experience.

Author's Note

Fairy Herbs for Fairy Magic is a practical resource about the use of plant materials which are perfectly synergistic with a fairy-based or fairy-related spiritual path.[1] As such, the book is structured in three parts followed by Appendixes A, B, and C.

Part 1 examines the meaning of fairy faith, fairy magic, and fairy familiars. The history of partnerships between humans and fairies, what kind of herbal knowledge was offered by fairy familiars and how exactly such knowledge was imparted are also overviewed Part 1 concludes with a guided meditation to meet a fairy ally whose main role is that of a guide into the practice of fairy-based spiritual herbalism.

Part 2 answers first the question, *what qualifies an herb as fairy herb?* It then offers a listing of about forty trees, resins, and herbs, their lore and uses in fairy-related magic. Special consideration is given in Part 2 to water from various sources and the role water plays in fairy spiritual herbalism and fairy herbal magic: snow water, dew, rainwater, and water from sacred wells are all discussed in detail.

Part 3 begins with some guidance about harvesting and harnessing plant energy, followed by a collection of practical recipes. Here the reader will find an assortment of charms for protection, abundance, attracting love, energetically cleansing people, spaces, and objects. There is ample guidance about warding against unwanted attention from malevolent fairy beings while simultaneously propitiating the presence of those fairy beings one wishes to partner up with, and suggestions on how to improve communication with fairy allies, etc.

Appendix A presents fairy gardens as part of one's spiritual personal practice and as means to honor fairy beings whose partnership one seeks to invite. Fairy gardens may be regarded as something modern, New Age-ish, but the practice of building houses and spaces especially intended for fairies has much older roots. Appendix A discusses what to take into consideration to recreate the practice in ways that are meaningful for us today.

In Appendix B the readers learn about an old Romanian ritual held to honor fairies and its adaptation to suit modern practitioners. A substantial list of suggested readings and resources is offered in Appendix C. All the material referenced in the book can be retrieved among the titles listed in Bibliography.

My own training, practice, and beliefs are bound to color what I write, and will unavoidably bring some degree of subjectivity. However, throughout the book there are clear specifications as to what information comes from what source, and my personal experiences will be explicitly labeled as such.

I shall emphasize that none of the material presented in *Fairy Herbs for Fairy Magic* is intended as medical advice or substitute for medical treatment. We caution against ingesting any herb without approval and supervision from properly trained health care practitioners who have the legal capacity to prescribe and advise in this regard.

That being said, I am now inviting you to follow along through meadows and forests, sit by murmuring springs and crystal-clear wells, learn from conversations between fairy witches and their fairy familiars, journey to meet your own fairy ally, and set forth on the path of herbal fairy magic.

Daniela Svartheiðrin Simina
December, 2022

Introduction

"Write the book you wish to read." This timeless piece of advice that will never go out of fashion, diminish in practicality, or lose veracity, has been one of the motivating factors that prompted me to write *Fairy Herbs for Fairy Magic*. This is the book I wish I had years ago, and this is still the book I want to have at hand today as a seasoned practitioner of plant energy medicine whose spiritual path is based in fairy beliefs. I have always thought it would be handy to have all the information neatly organized in one single volume, as opposed to looking up ten or twenty separate books and countless articles to piecemeal information that connects *specifically* plants and trees to fairy magic. I thought it would be nice, practical, time saving (and sanity-saving too!) not to spend hours retrieving information bit by bit each time I need it. Since I could not find such a book, I thought I'd write it myself.

Another reason for writing *Fairy Herbs for Fairy Magic* is the acute need for ushering fairy magic back into our overly technologized world and ways of living. This is something that lies at the core of my spiritual path and my work. In their book, *Living Fairy*, Morgan Daimler speaks about the importance of what they call re-enchanting the world. It can and it should be done, bringing back the wild and magic that is intrinsic to fairies and to the work of those who partner up with them.

> *...re-enchanting the mortal world. It's a concept that has been coming up in the last few years among different communities...My view has always been that to achieve this re-enchantment of the world we need to only change how we perceive it because there is plenty of enchantment already here. But experiences in Iceland in September 2018 have changed my understanding of several things including this subject. I believe now that it is essential that we*

do actively seek to bring the Other into our world and that it is essential for us to return our world to a state of balance with the Otherworld by opening the way again. (Daimler, 2020, p.2)

It is urgent that we bring back what was muffled and nearly lost in the process of aggressive industrialization, extreme materialistic thinking, and religious radicalism. These factors have precipitated our relationship with the wonders of the natural world and its magic and lead humankind to spiritual starvation thus setting it on the path to self-destruction. This message, about the need to re-enchant the world, to awaken an increasingly numb society is by no means proselytizing about returning to an idyllic past. (I shall digress to remind that there is nothing idyllic about crop maturation at the mercy of the elements, nor is anything idyllic about Middle Ages toilets.) This book is thus not a petition urging for a return to a past long-gone, but an invitation to learn from that past and leverage the knowledge to advance a fairy based-practice which is connected to what once was, yet perfectly suited for where we are today.

Mine is not a solitary effort. This book, as it is the case with my entire work,[2] makes up just a tiny thread in a tapestry where many other weaver-writers contributed their own threads. *Fairy Herbs for Fairy Magic* is part of the joint effort to bring back the enchantment along with the wild, fearsome, fiery, boisterous fairy magic. In her class "Elves and Witches: A Survival Guide", author and scholar Cat Heath talks in unequivocal terms about the necessity of restoring practices that pertain to elves and fairies.

They [elves and fairies] are important for this world. Every being suffers from their absence. They suffer from having been chased away. Colonization and Christianization drove out indigenous humans, and elves and fairies. (Heath, 2022)

Disenchantment of our world may hold different meanings for different people, but there is a common denominator for all the circulating iterations: the loss of wonder, a sense of disconnect, the sense of incompleteness and perennial dissatisfaction that affects many despite professional success and acquisition of wealth, are all to be reckoned with. (Beckett, 2015) It is stringent to understand that disenchantment is a real problem and it affects us all. Once disenchantment is understood and acknowledged as a real problem, we can move on to restore the enchantment in the world we live in, to bring back what has been lost.

> *We actually need serious restoration, not only re-enchantment.* *(Seo Helrune, 2018)*

Bringing back fairy magic involves creating fairy partnerships. To form long-lasting partnership one needs to take the time to learn about fairies, which implies studying fairy lore both past and present. Society evolves and knowledge changes – this holds true for both sides, humans and fairies. Neither humans nor fairies are stuck in time, fossils from a past long gone. Things change and the body of lore evolves to reflect the change. It is important to know how fairy-related practices were in the past not because we shall repeat the past *ad litteram*, but because it gives us a better understanding of how practices, beliefs, and traditions have evolved, and what mistakes to avoid. I will repeat here something I wrote and said on different occasions, something I believe holds true today more than ever. Learning from the lore that reaches us from both distant and not so distant past helps us to better understand fairies in the present. The quality of our relationships depends on the degree of understanding, and the degree of understanding depends on what and how much we read, study, and experience. *Fairy Herbs for Fairy Magic'* presents a synthesis of old material and material that reflects more modern views of witchcraft and fairies, together with the author's personal experience. It is a guide intended to facilitate the work of those called to a fairy path by adding in fairy-guided herbalism.

There is no pretense or claim that the information presented in *Fairy Herbs for Fairy Magic* is some sort of "ultimate truth" with nothing left to be said or discovered beyond what is written here. Essentially, this book is not an ultimate destination, the place where everything is being spelled out (pun fully intended) in a definitive manner, but something for the reader to leverage and use to further connect with fairies as guides and allies. The purpose? Answering this question takes us all the way back to the discussion about the need to re-enchant the world, a need that is more acute today than it has ever been.

Part 1

Fairies and Fairy Partnerships

Chapter 1

Fairies

Fairy is a word adopted to describe a supernatural being regardless of culture. (Heath, 2022)

In the context of this book fairies are understood as beings who inhabit the Otherworld, a world that is parallel, even adjacent, to the human world and copiously bleeding into it in various places and at different times. Fairies, the ones referred to in this book, are otherworldly beings, humanoid-looking to various degrees, having different sizes, and possessing abilities that can be labeled magic. All fairies can acquire different degrees of corporality and are capable of shapeshifting into animal, bird, and any other form. All fairy beings can be contacted expressly by humans, or they stumble into people's lives especially when the human in question undergoes some sort of crisis. (Wilby, 2006) Fairies and fairy-like beings are present in every culture under various names.

There are many ways to classify fairies, far too many to attempt all here. Fairies are too elusive to lend themselves to precise categorization and this often clashes against humans' irresistible urge to organize everything into more or less elaborate taxonomies. While classifications and taxonomies can be useful to understand relationships or relative positions, artificial criteria imposed on beings such as fairies could be more detrimental than useful. What follows is not really a classification but a broad overview of fairies as they appear in different contexts. Such an overview is helpful in understanding human-fairy partnerships as they are discussed further in this chapter.

Modern theories rooted in the Theosophical movement[3] ascribes fairy beings to the air, water, fire, and spirit categories, categorizing them as elementals. Accordingly, fairies do not exist outside these categories, and whatever does is not a fairy. I personally encountered people arguing vehemently that elementals are *the only* true fairies. This interpretation has no real foundation and it is not supported by evidence from any lore, in any culture. Rather, while elements such as water, air, earth, and fire might be understood as having their own spirits or elementals which could be seen as fairies (with the specification that fairies in this context is being used as an umbrella term), not all fairies are elementals (Daimler, 2014).

I personally side with the belief that there is a distinction between nature spirits and fairies per se. Genius loci is *the* spirit of a certain place or natural feature. It is attached to the place and it does not change residence. Fairies often claim an area or a natural feature for themselves so their presence could be ascertained in addition to that of the existing genius loci. Some places and landscape features such as specific rocks, certain solitary trees, groves, hillocks, and caves, are residence to fairies or act as portals between their world and ours. Fairies may act as guardians of those places and features because it is their territory after all but they do not replace the genius loci. Fairies can leave while the spirit of the place, the genius loci, is as permanent as the place itself. Among those who play the role of guardians of various natural features, only some are fairies. This does not imply that fairy beings are not connected to the land and landscape in more profound ways. Accounts from Icelandic lore tell that upon their arrival in Iceland, humans came in contact with land wights. Having agency over land fertility and weather, Icelandic wights helped the first human communities to survive and eventually thrive. (Gundarsson, 2007) There are many stories about farmers receiving help from elves and wights dwelling in large boulders or other features in the landscape. The help ceased and the farmers' luck ran out when elves or wights were chased away by the holy water sprinkled over their boulder-residences by Christian priests. (Gundarsson, 2007; Sigmundsdottir, 2021)

In Ireland, certain solitary hawthorns are known to be fairy residences or serve as portals to the fairy world. Damaging such trees would result in terribly bad luck, even death. A similar fate awaits those who would disturb mounds known to belong to fairies whether ancient burial mounds or naturally occurring hillocks. (Lenihan, 2004) Romanian fairy lore is filled with cautionary tales about humans disrespecting fairy places and paying with their health or life. (Simina, 2023). Norse, Germanic, and Anglo-Saxon records mention the practice of placing offerings under the first furrow to propitiate the spirits responsible with land fertility. (Heath, 2022) In Christianized garb, the old practice of offering to the land wights and elves survived as did peoples' belief in these beings.

In Romanian, Irish, Norse and Germanic cultures, fairies and the dead overlap to a significant degree. There are stories of humans believed to be dead but actually appearing to relatives to tell them that they have been abducted into Fairy. Stories about The Hunt and the Wild Hunt are common to Irish, Germanic and Norse lore. In these stories people who encounter the dangerous fairy processions oftentimes recognize relatives or people they once knew among procession participants. This aspect of fairy identity is important when considering the links to ancestors. In this context making offerings to fairies acquires another layer of meaning.

Corpus material about fairies mentions them appearing to humans for various reasons and in various circumstances. In many such stories, fairies appear to live lives similar to humans' and confront similar problems. Irish and Romanian lore, for example, tell about fairy women asking for milk or flour, sometimes only to test the generosity of the human counterpart. Fairies borrow or steal cattle, and either ask mortal women to help delivering babies or abduct midwives and wet-nurses. Stories tell about fairy men borrowing tools from humans when theirs break down, and rewarding handsomely the person who help them fix the broken equipment. Some fairies are hostile to humans and interacting with them can be outright dangerous. First line of defense is to be as well informed as possible about the fairy beings one could encounter in specific areas which implies the usefulness of reading the lore and listening to native stories. If one needs to interact with fairies, showing character and good manners are of paramount importance.

Chapter 2

Fairy Faith and Fairy Magic

Fairy Faith

As it is mentioned in this text, fairy faith simply means the belief in the existence of fairies. More beliefs about fairies aggregate around faith in their existence contributing to each person's understanding of them. Further, understanding has an influence on peoples' fairy-related experiences.

I do not subscribe to the anthropocentric view of fairies that implies their purpose in a greater scheme of things as satellites to humans. Lore from various places, Irish, Romanian, Germanic, Icelandic, etc. picture relationships that range from random generosity, to reciprocity, to fairies plainly using humans for their own purposes. (O'Brien, 2021; Lenihan, 2004; Kligman, 1981; Gundarsson, 2007; Heath, 2022) Typically, when fairy beings offer help to humans, as we'll see in case of fairy familiars, there's always something expected in return. This picture is quite remote from the New Age view of fairies placed in service to humankind. Old lore does not present fairies in any way subservient to humans. It is not how nature works. Oak trees, for example, simply exist. It is not the purpose of oaks to feed the wildlife with their acorns, nor is their purpose to shelter nesting birds. Oaks produce acorns which they shed in fall. Wild boars feed on acorns because they find them on the forest floor, not because the oak purposefully disposes of acorns to feed the boars. Oaks have not been "designed" to take care of the boars' nutritional needs. Or, oaks have a reputation for attracting lightning: this does not imply that oaks have been intended by some god as lightning rods. Like oaks, fairies simply are.

Fairy Magic

When mentioning fairy magic, I have in mind two different yet closely related meanings. One refers to fairy magic as the magic done by the fairies themselves, their own ability to heal, influence luck, etc. The other connotation is that of magic done by people with fairy help or as taught by fairies. It is the magic performed by fairy seers, fairy witches, fairy doctors – however these practitioners are called within their own cultures. For example, in Icelandic lore Álf seiðr can be understood to refer to the magic practiced by elves, but can also describe the magic practiced by witches who work in partnership with elves. (Gundarsson, 2007; Heath, 2022)

Chapter 3

Fairy Familiars and Partnerships with Fairies

While recent years have witnessed an increase in fairies' expressed interest in interacting with humans matched by humans' willingness to engage, this phenomenon is not an absolute premiere. It would be safe to assume that humans reaching out to fairies and fairies reaching out to humans runs back farther than recorded history. In the absence of written sources, there isn't really a way to tell with certainty what shape these encounters and partnerships had, say, three thousand years ago. However, it would be safe to assume that partnerships between humans and fairies survived in the memory of the human species as they developed from the prehistoric roots and survived through thousands of years in the oral traditions, along with myths, sagas, and genealogies.

Even closer to our times, information about people working in partnership with fairies is quite abundant. Unfortunately, the source of such information is the grim reality of the persecution incurred by alleged witches and folk healers, especially women, during the witch hunt craze that swept Europe from the fifteenth into the eighteenth century. Albeit, extracted under torture and tainted by the bias of those who recorded court procedures and interrogatories, the victims' confessions reveal many trustworthy and therefore priceless details about the connection between witches and their fairy helpers. It is beyond the scope of this book to get into details about the infamous trials. For our purposes, suffice to say that all confessions reach common denominators in describing the fairy-witch relationships being based in reciprocity, having onset when the humans involved went through substantial crises, and delivering tangible benefits like healing and retrieving lost or stolen property (Wilby, 2006).

Another source that allows glimpsing into fairy-human partnerships is information preserved in the fairy lore and folklore from various cultures. For example, a large number of Irish traditions, customs, and stories related to fairies are recorded in the School Collection.[4] In Romania, fairy traditions survived the dictatorial regime (1945–1989) by keeping a low profile or masquerading as theatrical performance (Simina, 2022). Fairies, and the healing knowledge learned with aid from fairies moved once again in the foreground, after the Iron Curtain fell.

The so called "traditional" or popular medicine—including the clairvoyance—became acceptable and even fashionable. This happened simultaneously as the downfall of the communist regime and the beginning of the wars which accompanied its decomposition. (Vivod, 2014)

In Romania after 1989, the unpublished work of scholars along with materials produced by researchers from abroad brought to the public's attention the reality and continuity of fairy folklore and traditions. A relatively large corpus of material from Eastern and Southern Europe (which includes Romania) focuses on the practice of folk healers who allegedly work in partnership with fairy guides. Researchers have brought into the spotlight not only the lore of the centuries past but also the living traditions as they occur in the twentieth and twenty-first centuries (Pócs 1989; Kligman 1981; Vivod, 2014, 2018).

Stories about witches, folk healers, and ordinary people, who are not superficially interacting but engaging in long-term partnerships with fairies, are preserved in Germanic and Norse literature. Myths, sagas, old texts, and recent iterations, preserve knowledge and seed ideas about what partnerships with fairies – specifically elves and wights in this case – were like (Gundarsson,1993, 2007; Heath, 2021, 2022; Sigmundsdottir, 2021).

According to sources both old and new, partnerships with fairies typically commence when the human in question goes through a major crisis. From Bessie Dunlop's witch trials records[5] we learn that one day, as Bessie was walking across a field, a fairy man approached her. Bessie was in utter distress: one of her cows had died (it may feel trivial today, but in the 1500s the wellbeing and even survival for a farmer's family could depend on the very existence of that cow), her newborn baby was sick, her husband was ill with no perspective of recovery, and she herself was still weak after giving birth to her youngest child. Bessie had therefore every reason to feel desperate. As she later told interrogators, that was the moment when a fairy man appeared on the path in front of her and asked why she was crying; and so began Bessie Dunlop's partnership with Tom Reid, her fairy helper, or as known from trial records, her fairy familiar.

Sometimes fairy helpers appear when a person, not necessarily in a state of distress, makes an active effort to connect. The fairy beings who answer the call may be only temporary guides, or will become fairy familiars. This last one is usually a forever connection, unless the person renounces, denounces, or in some way offends the familiar who might leave for good.

Temporary guides may lead the querent to meet their familiar among fairies, or it may be the case that one or several among the temporary guides will stick around and grow into the role of fairy familiars. Fairies, whether familiars or temporary guides and allies, might appear on their own initiative or on behalf of a higher power such as a fairy monarch or deity.

As the name itself suggests, the fairy familiar is very close to the human they partner up with. The word closeness describes deep levels of connection such as the ones shared among family members or blood relatives. Closeness can also imply fairies and witches becoming involved as lovers and even spouses.

Fairy familiars can take different shapes: the best known are cats and dogs, but they could be anything from birds to wolves to creatures displaying mixed traits. They are not to be mistaken for pets or with any domestic cats and dogs which a folk healer or witch could have around the household (Daimler, 2011). Fairy allies, guides, or familiar may also appear in human form.

As already mentioned, another defining trait for human-fairy relationships is reciprocity. As Cat Heath explained in her class "Elves and Witches: A Survival Guide", relationships with otherworldly beings are not strictly transactional, elf vending machines where one drops an offering at one end and a boon is coming out at the other end. Reciprocity in relationships with fairies is far more nuanced than this. It takes time to build the relationship and to learn how to communicate clearly and unequivocally.

All practitioners of fairy-based folk medicine have one or more fairy allies or familiars and they reciprocate to these allies in various ways for the help received. Fairy-based folk medicine people are usually bound by oaths or promises, or must adhere to certain rules and lifestyle,[6] if Reciprocity can be expressed through offerings. Every culture mention making offerings to fairies. Usually offerings consist of food which is left in specific places on various occasions. Romanian folklore mentions the custom of making offerings to fairies in conjunction with different holidays, such as May Day, on their eponymous holiday, Sânziene, which occurs on Midsummer. Irish lore mentions food left out overnight for fairies. Norse texts speak of offerings made to the Álfar both whenever their help was sought after, and during the Álfablót, a dedicated celebration for which we have accounts but not a precise date (Gundarsson, 2007).

Offerings are not just about food. One can dedicate to them art, music, poetry, studying their lore, embodying in everyday life the principles and qualities that fairies much appreciate such as generosity, honesty, courage, and truthfulness.

It may seem complicated. But it is also worthwhile. So, before even taking any steps toward actively engaging with fairies, pause and ask yourself: what is your motivation? Why do you desire to have a fairy guide? Are you willing to get involved with a fairy familiar? Are you ready to shoulder the commitment? What can you offer, what can you contribute to the relationship?

Fairy witches, fairy, doctors, fairy seers – they have been known to play a role in society from remote past into present time. Some became well-known through the testimonies given during witch trials; some acquired great reputation in their lifetime and they are still spoken about in reverent tones years after they left this world. Yet others serve their communities today, sought after by both people in need for their help and by researchers seeking to document fairy folk healers.

In the article "The Witch, the Bean Feasa, and the Fairy Doctor in Irish Culture" Morgan Daimler explains the connection between certain Irish practitioners of folk medicine and fairies.

In modern American terms we tend to call anyone who works with low magic or folk magic a witch; however, from an Irish perspective such people actually fell into roughly three groups: witches called cailli (singular cailleach) in Irish, fairy doctors, and mná feasa (singular ban feasa). It is important to note up front that all three of these terms can be and sometimes are used interchangeably, and a single person may be given all three labels by different people. (Daimler, 2014)

It is dangerous to overly generalize and indiscriminately paint with exceedingly wide brushes all fairy witches or practitioners of folk medicine who work with fairies. Daimler's description captures the essence. Commonly, practitioners of fairy-based folk medicine from across cultures provide healing by using remedies and knowledge given by fairies. They help retrieve lost or stolen property using information provided by fairy helpers, protect against fairy mischief, and heal ailments caused by inimical fairies. Here is a small sample of what we know about the activity of fairy healers and witches and the ways they received knowledge and herbs from their fairy allies.

Bessie Dunlop (Scotland, seventeenth century) received from Tom Reid, her familiar, recipes for herbal prescriptions to cure certain ailments. For example, in the case of a noble woman suffering from fainting spells, Tom advised Bessie to give "…ginger, cloves, aniseeds, liquorice, and strong ale, seeth together, strain, and put in a vessel with white refined sugar" (Wilby, 2006). The remedy worked very well, and Bessie's reputation swelled.

Ann Jefferies, a Cornish witch who also lived in the seventeenth century, was known for her ability to heal through laying of hands and by using herbal salves made upon instructions received from fairies (Young, 2021).

In Ireland, nineteenth century bean feasa (wise woman), Eibhlin Ní Ghuinníola, had a fairy lover who was seen by other people accompanying her while gathering herbs (Daimler, 2014; O Crualaoich, 2003).

Biddy Early is, beyond any shade of a doubt, the best-known fairy doctor in Ireland. She was reputed for her blue bottle, a gift from fairies, that she consulted to provide advice and cures to those seeking her help. Aside from the blue bottle, on at least one occasion Biddy is known to have used an herb, Lady's Fingers or Lady's Bedstraw to effect a cure. (Lenihan, 1987) Biddy was perceived by some as being not only in a relationship with fairies, but also a fairy herself. This points to yet another possible layer of connection between fairies and those who work with them.

They made out that she was a witch an' fairy for what she was doing. (Lenihan, 1987, p.93)

Ivanka is a fairy-seer who lives in a Romanian-speaking community in present-day Serbia. In her quality as the subject of a documentary realized in 2018 by Maria Vivod, PhD, Ivanka talks openly about the importance of her role in the community and details her going into trance and working with fairies.[7] As seen in the recorded footage, while dancing her way into trance, Ivanka holds a sprig of basil, an herb long associated with magic in Eastern European folklore. Ivanka mentions pear trees as being special to fairies, and she tells how she was taken numerous times up a pear tree by the three fairies she works for (Vivod, 2018).

Chapter 4

Connecting and Communicating with Fairy Guides

Connecting with the Fairy Guides

If you are already working with fairies, and are well established in fairy witchcraft, and the only thing that you seek is adding the herbalism dimension to your practice, then the next paragraph could be somewhat of a review. But, if you are relatively new to working with fairies or just figuring out your path, then read carefully and by no means limit yourself to apprehending only what's written here. For a solid foundation in fairy witchcraft or any form of fairy partnership you might envision, I strongly suggest that you consult Morgan Daimler's *Fairy Witchcraft*, and if you are drawn toward Germanic and Norse elves, then Cat Heath's *Elves, Witches & Gods* is an essential foundation piece.

Generally speaking, if you seek out fairy partnerships, then make sure you get on their good side by following some general rules of conduct:

- Be aware of what culture your specific fairy beings are related to, like Irish, Icelandic, English, Romanian, etc., and read all the lore you can find about them. You cannot understand people outside their own culture; and fairies *are* people.

- Don't act entitled. You seek out partners, not servants. Drop the homocentric view about mankind as the superior beings entitled to everything. It is this mentality that brought us where we are today, on the brink of self-destruction and begging for fairies to return. Read Seo Helrune post "Restoration, Not Re-Enchantment" listed in Appendix C, Resources, for details.

- Get to know as well as possible the fairies you seek to connect with, take time to introduce yourself properly, make yourself a pleasant neighbor to them, before asking for anything.
- Be polite.
- Do not commit to anything that is binding in a forever-like fashion. Binding contracts made with fairies are nearly impossible to dissolve and are always drafted with their own interest coming first.
- When in doubt, ask questions. Saying "I'm not sure", "I don't understand", "I need more time to think of this", "What are the implications of...." buys time to understand the situation, ponder over choices, and avoid saying no in a way that could be offensive to them.
- Make offerings.
- Respect their places: **do not** take souvenirs from ancient monuments or trees. Aside from being plainly destructive, there are many horror stories about what happened to people who damaged or otherwise disrespected fairy property. If you are curious about such stories, Eddie Lenihan's *Otherworldly Encounters* will give you a taste.
- Fairies don't lie, and abhor being lied to. Don't make promises that you cannot keep. While it is true that fairies don't lie, they are masterful with words and can tweak what they say to sound like something you may want to hear while actually meaning something entirely different. Ask questions before committing to anything. Run everything by your fairy guide, (the meditation at the end of this chapter leads you to encounter your fairy guide) and/or consult the gods connected to fairies in their specific cultures. For example, I have a strong connection with An Dagda who is also known in the lore as king of all fairies in Ireland. I place myself under his protection each time I go to Ireland and whenever I venture into

uncharted waters where I am likely to encounter sí (Irish fairies) that I don't know and of whose intentions I'm not certain.

- Keep in touch with your fairy guide, or guides. Communicate often. The more people talk to each other the better they get to know one another. Which takes us straight to the next important aspect, that of communicating with fairies.

Communicating with Fairies

Having read about fairy healers who meet their familiars as corporeal beings, you may feel intimidated and thoughts of inadequacy may be creeping in. Do not worry. Some among the most proficient healers and fairy witches that I know do not see their familiars and guides as 3D manifestations. Some fairy witches just sense the presence of their fairy allies, hear them, or take clues from the environment about their presence. The fact that you don't see fairies or experience them as corporeal beings does not mean that you cannot communicate with them. Fairy allies reach out in several ways:

- Meditation and journey– If you do not have a meditation practice, it would be a good idea to establish one. Personally, I believe in meditation that is done not only for the sake of meditation but for the usefulness of it. Being able to relax, focus, and possibly visualize are great assets when seeking to interact with fairies. But visualization itself is not mandatory, so just relax, focus, and pick clues on any channel that is more naturally developed in you. Different people rely on different senses to psychically retrieve information. For example, you may be more clairaudient rather than visual and get messages in some auditory form. You may hear the voices of your fairy allies as if coming from outside yourself or you may hear them as thoughts that form in your own head, or as ideas that you can surely recognize as not being your own.

- Dreams– It is a good idea to monitor your dreams, especially when you have questions for your fairy allies and are asking them to get in touch with you via dreams. Fairies may have suggestions or specific requests for you about what or how to do things in ritual, for example. Post-ritual, it is possible for you to receive messages in dreams that could provide answers to various questions, hint at how effective the ritual has been, etc.

- Omens– You may want to look for omens. You can get an idea about fairy presence around you by taking clues from the environment. In time you may find out that specific occurrences, for example, noticing a certain scent that you have no logical explanation for, may correlate with fairy presence. Not all birds, pretty flowers, or particular cloud patterns signal that your fairy allies are around or that they have taken note of your request for help. Most of the time a hawk landing on the tree next to you is nothing but a hawk landing on a tree. However, if hawks are rare in your area and you see one landing nearby, shortly after you petitioned your fairy ally, or when you have just asked for an omen, then you might consider the hawk to be a sign of fairies paying attention. So it is very important that you are connected to your environment and know what is a trivial occurrence and what is not.

- Divination– You can communicate with fairies through divination tools. Anything that you feel comfortable with will do. Start with whatever you have at hand: cards, runes ogham, reading tea leaves. In time, fairies will find ways to even tell you what tool they prefer that you use for this purpose. It may be a pendulum made in a certain way, a specific deck of cards, runes made from a material of their specification – the possibilities are virtually infinite. I have a friend who was told by her fairy guide to use bones to communicate with her fairy allies. Shortly after having received the message, while strolling in the woods, my friend found on the ground a bunch of small animal bones and she instinctively knew they would be the perfect tool. She poured out fresh water as an offering to the spirit of the animal whose bone she collected, and then poured some more water expressing gratitude to fairies who guided her to the bones. She cleansed the bones, dedicated them through ceremony, and has been using these exclusively to communicate with her fairy allies. Which gets me to the next point: I strongly recommend having a dedicated tool to use just for interacting with fairies. My Ælfe guides asked for a set of runes made of apple wood, and I am not to use the specific rune set for anything outside of connecting with them. To work with clients or conduct inquiries for myself I use a separate set of runes made of deer antlers.

That little voice in your head… You should learn to trust it. The only way to learn to trust your intuition is through training, to recognize its voice among the million other voices all fighting for your attention at any given moment. Which brings us back full circle: the best way to train your attention, concentration, and refine your perception and intuition – all at the same time – is through meditation.

Meditation to Contact Your Fairy Guide

If you never worked with a fairy guide before, this is a safe enough, and simple enough introduction. If you already have experience with journeying and contacting fairy allies, then take this as an opportunity to try something different, something that I hope you will enjoy enough to use again in the future.

In this meditation, you will travel to the liminal space between this world and the Other to meet a fairy guide who is directly and specifically connected to fairy herbal magic. This is your fairy ally that is ready and willing to connect with you at this specific time. This is the fairy guide who can show you the ropes of fairy herbal medicine. This guide that you are about to meet could be a short term, long term, or permanent connection: time will tell.

The pronoun 'they' is used instead of 'she' or 'he', so you will not be subliminally biased about who appears in front of you. Also, is it very possible for your fairy guide to appear as a gender neutral being in which case the pronoun 'they' fits better than gendered pronouns. By no means would we want to objectify fairy allies and refer to them as 'it'; it would be utterly disrespectful.

I would suggest familiarizing yourself with the script before actually diving into meditation. You may record yourself reading the meditation so you can play it back to yourself whenever you wish to use it. Or have someone else read the text while you journey.

You can use this meditation not only when you need advice about your herbal practice but whenever you would like to chit chat with your guide. Once you get familiar with the format, feel free to change this script and adapt it to suit your taste and style of practice.

Sit comfortably or lay down if you prefer. Cover up with a blanket, or if you do have a dedicated cloak that you use for journey and meditation work, don that instead. Cover your eyes; make sure that light is not a distraction.

Take the deepest of breaths, hold the air in for a couple of seconds, then simply let the air flow out. Allow yourself to drop into the emptiness the outflowing breath left behind.

Don't rush to breathe in; only do so when it comes naturally.

Next time you breathe in, go slowly, and only stop when you feel your lungs comfortably full.

Pause at the top of your in-breath for just one second, then relax your abdomen and chest and let the air flow out.

Don't rush to breathe in, but wait for the natural impulse to guide you as to when to take in your next breath.

Breathe in slowly.

Hold briefly.

Breath out softly.

Pause.

Breathe in slowly.

Hold briefly

Breath out softly.

Pause.

Now allow the breath to settle and let go of any kind of breathing pattern, of any lengthening or breath retention.

Let the breath happen, and with each exhale fall back farther and deeper within yourself.

One more breath, and yet another.

Fall freely, float, spiral downward like a leaf carried away by wind.

One more breath, and yet another.

(Allow some time)

Your free-falling slows down…

It slows down until it comes to a full stop. You are now standing and feel there's solid ground beneath your feet although you can't see anything in the dense milky fog that surrounds you. The fog is dense, impenetrable to your sight but feels silky and pleasant to touch.

You begin to set one foot in front of the other, and step by step you advance on the path that feels sturdy beneath your feet. You feel safe and confident, knowing that your instinct is your compass, and that it takes you in the right direction.

The fog begins to thin out, and you distinguish the shapes of large trees surrounding you.

As you advance, the fog clears. You realize that you walk through a forest, more beautiful than any forest you ever saw. The trees are magnificent; their branches weave a thick canopy high above you. You might hear birds singing. Animals might swiftly cross your path.

You keep walking. You can't afford to get distracted now when you are about to meet your fairy ally in this liminal space between Worlds.

Ahead of you the path is ending, and you can see a clearing with a very large stone at its center.

From behind the stone, or maybe straight out of it, a silhouette emerges. It is someone who looks in your direction, clearly anticipating your arrival.

You wave and your guide waves back, motioning you to get closer.

As you draw near you become increasingly more aware of details that you couldn't get from afar. How does your fairy guide look? (Allow time for observation)

With a spring in your step you get near them, greet, introduce yourself, and explain what brings you here. (Allow time for introduction)

Ask your fairy guide their name. You may get a name, or maybe not, at least not yet. (Allow some time)

Ask them what herb they recommend that you work with at this time. They may name it or somehow show it to you. They will also tell you what the herb is for: maybe protection, maybe for healing of some sorts, maybe using it along with offerings. Just listen and watch. (Allow time for observation)

Ask your fairy guide what offerings would they enjoy, something you can give as a token of appreciation once you go back to the human world. If you hear anything you don't feel comfortable doing or giving, negotiate and agree upon something that is feasible for you and enjoyable for them. Your fairy guide may suggest a one-time offering or something to be done on a regular basis. (Pause. Allow some time)

You sense that the meeting has reached a conclusion. You bid farewell to your guide, and they bid you farewell in response. Do not rush. (Allow some time)

You turn around and walk away leaving the stone behind, knowing that you can return here whenever you wish.

You move quickly, and soon you step underneath the green canopy. (Allow time, about two or three breaths)

The sun is setting, shadows on the ground grow longer, and it is getting dark. (Allow some time)

The path is barely discernible in the moonless night, and soon darkness engulfs you completely.

The path vanishes from beneath your feet; you float again, riding the waves of your breath.

With each exhale you land back, more solidly, into your body.

With each inhale you become increasingly more aware of the form that you inhabit.

Take a few more breaths focusing on being present, on being fully back. (Allow time for three, maybe four breaths to fully process the return.)

When you feel ready, wiggle, stretch, and begin to move. Welcome back!

Ground yourself by eating something. Take a sip of water, juice, or tea. Most importantly, write down everything about your journey. These details will fade quickly and unless you record them you would miss important information.

Part 2

Fairy Herbs for Fairy Magic

Chapter 1

What Qualifies an Herb as a Fairy Herb?

Lore and anecdotal evidence speak unequivocally about fairies indicating or gifting specific herbs to people to use. Following such encounters, many among the humans involved gradually develop into fairy doctors, fairy witches, etc. however they are called within specific cultures.

We may have acquired by now an understanding of what is a fairy healer or a fairy witch. But what exactly is intended by fairy herbs to be used in fairy magic? What makes an herb a fairy herb?

> *And Tom would pull a herb and give it to her out of his own hand and bade her strain the same with any other kind of herbs and open the beast mouth and put them in and the beast would heal...*
> (Wilby, 2006)

I included in the fairy herbs category those plants that fairies themselves recommend to people for various uses. It is by no means implied that only fairies have knowledge of these herbs. It is intended, however, that fairies teach people about herbs they themselves feel comfortable with, herbs that do have an affinity with fairy nature. An exception to this rule is the situation when fairy familiars reveal knowledge of herbs that repel inimical fairy beings or heal ailments inflicted by fairies.

Fairies have their own preferences regarding herbs. Studying the lore and the experience built over time will inform what to use, when, and how. I added to the list those herbs known to be favored by fairies and which could invite their presence. Such herbs can be planted in designated spaces to honor fairy allies, their peoples, and propitiate positive interaction. Roses, whether planted or only dried petals, are a good example.

Some other herbs, outside those specifically recommended by fairies for various cures, are known for having intrinsic connections with the fairies themselves. For example, certain hawthorns are known to either be inhabited by fairies, or to act as a portal between this world and Fairy. Not every Hawthorn is a fairy tree, but since there are enough hawthorns known as fairy trees, by extension hawthorns in general bear associations to fairies. Fern is another such example. In the folklore of some cultures, ferns are said to hide entrances into fairy dwellings. Ferns are thus associated with fairy dwelling and passages into these without necessarily every fern concealing a door to a fairy home.

I also included in the list herbs whose folk-names specifically include the words fairy or elf, such as elf-leaf for lavender, elf wort for Elecampane or elven for Elm. While the extant lore about some of these plants is relatively scarce I still bring them to the readers' attention in an effort to preserve what is known no matter how little, and avoid even further loss of information.

Finally, herbs that have a banishing effect on certain types of fairies also make it into the list. Such herbs are connected to fairy in the sense that fairies dislike them profoundly and/or are adversely impacted by these herbs. For one reason or another, there are plants that fairies want to avoid at all costs. As we have already seen, fairy doctors and wise people working with fairy familiars are sometimes called to assist victims of unwanted fairy attention that resulted in disease and misfortune of all kinds. Certain plants are used in combination with other ingredients such as iron for a stronger banishing effect. I focus here on herbs that can create a filter-like protection, selectively allowing fairies who are well disposed toward the practitioner while repelling the inimical ones. Mugwort and Lady's Bedstraw are two such examples.

The next chapters will introduce trees, herbs and flowers, and tree-related materials such as resins to be used in fairy magic. There is also a short chapter on water. The inclusion of a chapter about water in a book that focuses on fairies and herbs may come as a surprise, but a closer analysis of source material and living traditions reveal a close connection between fairies, herbs, and water.

I personally believe that it is very important to know how the fairies that one seeks to connect with are portrayed in the native lore. This will help to weigh the pros and cons of using a specific type of plant and fine tune charms, spells, and rituals for the mutual benefit and enjoyment of practitioners and fairy allies.

Chapter 2

Trees

If you decide to use physical parts of trees in your practice, refrain from cutting bits and parts from them, unless it is the time for seasonal pruning or must eliminate branches that hang dangerously over your roof. Rely on wood that is ethically harvested and on parts that you can find fallen on the ground. Under no circumstances take samples from sacred trees growing on various sites. It is disrespectful to the fairies in the area, and it threatens the very existence of the tree. One leaf, or a tiny bit of bark may not seem to matter, but if one million people who visit a site take bits and pieces from a tree, the tree will soon disappear. The number, one million, is arbitrary: many sites, such as monuments in Ireland, receive over two million visitors per year, so please try to picture what this means.

Clootie trees as fairy trees are another big misunderstanding, and tying pieces of textiles to "clootie" trees has become the epitome of appropriation, selfishness, and ignorance. Clootie trees are trees growing adjoined to special places like wells or springs which were known for their healing powers. For hundreds, possibly thousands of years, clootie trees had been functioning as agents for healing. Originally, people tied bits of rags from a loved one's clothing while praying for their healing. It was thought that the disease left the person as the bit of fabric broke down. Countless trees have been damaged in Ireland by people tightly tying onto branches straps of every imaginable material or stick into the bark coins and pieces of jewelry. This is a mockery of the original belief, littering and vandalism combined, and is not going to bring any healing or wish fulfillment. It will instead bring the wrath of spirits guarding the place and the wrath of indigenous people witnessing the destruction of their beautiful trees. As far as fairies go, they are not going to be content, let alone reward anybody for littering and vandalizing trees. If you want to leave offerings to a fairy tree, leave water, bread, butter, fruit, or honey, all things that will not endanger wildlife nor the trees themselves. The food items mentioned are known to be enjoyed by a broad spectrum of fairy beings all across Europe. If you find yourself by a *real* clootie tree and wish to tie something onto it, tie a strip of paper (possibly with the name of the person you wish to heal), or a very light piece of natural fabric which will either disintegrate quickly in the elements or will break as the tree grows.

Let's now look at trees that in different bodies of lore appear to be connected to various kinds of fairies and fairy beings.

Apple
(Malus domestica, M. pumila, M. communi, Pyrus malus)
Echtra Condla, The Adventures of Connla The Fair, is one of the earliest Irish tales existing in manuscript form. The language in the manuscript has been traced back to the seventh century, but research indicates that the story itself is an iteration of much older lore. Echtra Condla is the earliest recorded story in Irish literature to feature a fairy protagonist. Noteworthy for our purposes, the connection between fairies and apples is at the forefront of the tale. The fairy woman in the story gives Connla an apple which becomes the only food he desires. Bits of apple were enough to satisfy Connla's hunger. It seems that the apple also added to the enchantment that made Connla wish for nothing else but to be with the fairy woman. It certainly makes this story an early record for apples' use in fairy love magic.

> *But as the woman departed before the potent chanting of the druid, she threw Connla an apple. Connla remained to the end of the month without food or drink ...save only the apple. What he ate*

of the apple never diminished it...Longing seized upon Connla for the woman he had seen. (Echtra Condla, Lebor Na hUidre, Mary Jones Celtic Literature Collective)

The fairy woman took Connla to Tír na nÓg, The Land of the Young, also named Emhain Abhlach, the Island/Place of Apples. In Irish myth the Island of Apples is a place that belongs to fairies. It is related to eternal youth, and obviously, to apples. Manannán Mac Lir, sea god who is also a fairy king, rules there. Manannán helped the Tuatha Dé Danann to adapt to living inside the sí mounds after the Milesians took over in Ireland.

The Irish epic, Táin Bó Cúailnge, The Cattle Raid of Cooley, mentions the Irish god Lugh as one of the fairies (Gantz, 1982). In Cath Maige Tuired, The Battle of Moytura, Lugh is leading the fairy cavalcade. (https://celt.ucc.ie/). Lugh was raised on Emhain Abhlach having Mannán as his foster father. To punish those who killed his biological father, Lugh sends them away to bring him a magical apple from a place underneath the sea. The said apple has the color of gold, it tastes like honey, it heals wounds and diseases, satiates hunger, and never finishes no matter how much one eats from it: which description connects the said apple to the Tír na nÓg and the realm of Fairy (Mac Coitir, 2018).

Manánan owns a magical silver branch with nine golden apples so irresistibly alluring that king Cormac mac Airt is willing to trade anything to obtain it. The golden apples play beautiful music when the branch is shaken. The music makes one forget all sorrows and weariness (Jacobs, 1894). Apple magical power as described here, accomplishes emotional healing.

The Irish hero, Blaiman, Son of Apple, was conceived when his mother ate the only apple that grew on an apparently magical tree. "He was born with a golden spot on his poll and a silver spot on his head and very beautiful in form" (Mc Coitir, 2018, p.87). This story is just one example speaking of apples related to the ability to conceive through magical means.

Norse myth talks about goddess Iðunn who owns a basket with apples that grant the Æsir, Norse gods, eternal youth. Iðunn herself is from among the Vanir, the other major group of gods in Norse mythology. In the Poetic Edda, Iðunn is mentioned as being related to the elves (Sturlusson,1995). The elements in Iðunn's lore thus assemble to convey apples' association with youth, vitality, and magical powers of the elves.

In Romanian fairy lore, the fairy man, Fāt Frumos, Handsome Lad, is on a quest to retrieve some magical golden apples from an enchanted garden. The apples grant great beauty and health to whoever eats from them (Ispirescu, 2016). Romanian folklore also mentions apple trees related to the magic of fairies. The motif of apple sprigs that have the power to bring the dead back to life appears in the story of Harap Alb, White Moor, where a fairy woman uses three apple sprigs and spring water to resuscitate the protagonist. In this case too, the apple ushers in romantic love. Harap Alb and the fairy woman fall in love with each other and get married (Creangā, 2008).

There is a lot in the source material that indicates apples as appropriate offerings for fairies. The offering aspect depends on the cultural context, and while generally speaking one can't go wrong offering apples, it never hurts to closely research what is customary within the culture or pantheon that you personally connect with.

Irish lore mentions Manannán appearing in the guise of a fool or jester playing tricks, performing fits of magic, and playing the most amazing music on his harp. He would accept no payment but sour milk and apples (Mac Coitir, 2018). This example makes the case for dairy and apples as offerings appreciated by a fairy king, Manannán himself.

Romanian fairies have an affinity for apple and pear trees. Offerings for them are often left by these trees. Apples themselves are part of offerings made to ancestors on the feast day of Rusalii, powerful Romanian fairies known for their ambivalence in relationship to humans. The holiday of Rusalii has been incorporated into the Christian observance of Pentecost. The ancient ritual dances performed on this occasion have survived, and so did the custom of offering food – apples featuring prominently – to fairies and ancestors.

The material discussed so far makes it evident that apple trees are generally resonant with fairy beings. Apple twigs can be used in magic related to health, both physical and emotional. The fruit is suited for love magic, charms for youthfulness, beauty, fertility, and also health and healing. Incorporated in charms, apples can propitiate the presence of fairy allies. They also make good offerings.

Use apple wands in spells and rituals for wellbeing, attractiveness, and fertility. Wear apple seeds and/or dried bits of apples in charms (small pouches, satchels) to bolster health and wellbeing. If you are seeking to conceive, wear apple seeds in charms consecrated for this purpose. Use apple wands in rituals where fairies are honored or their presence propitiated. See Part 3 for healing, fertility, beauty, and attractiveness spells and charms

Ash

(Fraxinus excelsior, F. americana)

In Norse mythology, Yggdrasil, the World Tree, is believed to be an ash tree (alternatively, yew or possibly apple). Nine realms aggregate around Yggdrasil, with Alfheim, the realm of Elves, being one of them. Yggdrasil is therefore indissolubly connected to the Elves and suited for use in elf magic. Ash twigs or a piece of wood can be used to emulate Yggdrasil in rituals, and 'bridge' the way for eleven allies to come along. Yggdrasil's roots reach all the way down into Niflheimr, the realm of the dead, and its top reaches all the way up to Asgard, the place of gods. This is a relevant detail for those working with fairy beings from the Norse tradition, because a) there is a significant degree of overlap between the human dead and the elves epitomized in the story about a human king who became an elf after dying and continued to live in the mound where he was buried; (Sturluson, 1990) and b) among the gods in Asgard several, like Freya, Iðunn, and Oðin himself, have different degrees of connection with the elves (Sturlusson,1990, Heath, 2021). It is thus rather logical to think of ash as supportive of communication with elves from all across the breadth of the spectrum covered by Yggdrasil.

Irish lore also connects ash to fairy beings, with ash facilitating the ability to see fairies. Traditions suggest making a loop from an ash twig and watching through it to see fairies dancing. (Wild, 1991)

Use ash twigs to cast circles or otherwise mark ritual spaces where you intend to communicate with fairy beings. Ash will facilitate communicating with the elves, and based on my experience, with other kinds of fairies too. Wear a small ash amulet (few leaves, a bit of bark, the tiniest of sticks) and be very clear about who you are inviting in your ritual space. Never put out blanket invitations because you don't know who might answer, and not all fairies are fond of humans.

Ash adds power to your intentions in regard to both fairies who you seek to invite and fairies you want to keep out. The power of ash in conjunction with that of your focused intent creates a selective barrier that allows your fairy allies in, while keeping the troublesome ones out of your ritual space. In Part 3, you will find instructions on how to make charms to propitiate fairy presence while at the same time keeping you safe. Please bear in mind that safety is always a relative term when dealing with fairies, and good manners are of paramount importance.

Birch

(Betula alba, B. pendula, B. pubescens, B. lenta)

In Europe, birch is generally known to protect against malevolent spirits and for its connection to purification and healing. In fairy witchcraft, birch is not a fairy repellent per se, but it can be added to charms aimed to protect against unwanted attention from mischievous fairies and reverse diseases caused by them.

Birch brooms can be used to cleanse and hallow the ritual space before inviting in fairy allies. Considering birch's ability to offer protection selectively, it enables you to bring into the ritual space those fairies who are goodly inclined and keep out the others. Mound elves and land wights favor birch, so if your allies are from among these fairy beings, using birch in ritual will propitiate their presence (Gundarsson, 2007).

Birch, whether added to herbal satchels or used in the form of essential oil, is excellent for cleansing oneself after visiting fairy places through journey work or after contact with places in physical reality where the energy felt particularly heavy.

For fairy doctors, fairy witches, or fairy seers who do spiritual healing, cleansing baths in which birch is used is essential part of selfcare (Daimler, 2016). Use birch regularly to avoid the side effects of energetic contamination. See Part 3 for suggestions on how to prepare cleansing baths and techniques for purification from diseased energy.

Blackthorn

(Prunus spinosa)

Blackthorn is one among several trees that can offer selective protection. Same as the hawthorn that is discussed further in this section, the blackthorn tree is a fairy favorite. Scottish and Irish lore mention a specific type of fairy, the lunantishee, that is connected to the blackthorn and will punish whoever harms this tree (Mac Coitir, 2018). Not all blackthorns are fairy trees, but one should treat them with respect regardless: better safe than sorry. In Ireland, the wood of the blackthorn tree is fashioned into shillelaghs, walking sticks that also function as formidable weapons. The connection to weaponry and the fact that its thorns can inflict painful wounds that heal slowly and with difficulty, makes blackthorn well suited for defense magic, as well as cursing. I personally have a close, long standing relationship with blackthorn and I rely on its qualities whenever needed.

Mark the boundaries of your ritual space by walking around with either a shillelagh or a blackthorn wand, and ask the Blackthorn spirit to protect your space. If you are aware of negative magic directed your way, wear a protection charm that has a blackthorn thorn in it. See Part 3 for details on how to use blackthorn for protection.

Elder
(Sambucus nigra, S. canadensis)

Elder has a contradictory nature and ambivalent energy which makes it relatively complicated to work with. Elder is related to healing, in medicinal herbalism and healing magic, but also to cursing. It is connected to fairies and invites their presence. Elder can also be used for protection against malevolent fairies and repel other harmful energies such as curses. If used by someone who does not resonate well with this tree, defense magic involving elder could backfire. Damaging an elder tree or harvesting wood from one without properly showing respect attracts misfortune.

Old lore from Western Europe describes the spirit of the elder tree as an old woman. The "Elder Mother" must be asked for permission before cutting wood from an elder tree (Mac Coitir, 2018; Daimler, 2015; Cunningham. 1985). I believe that it is even better to propitiate her good will with offerings. Elder is well known for its association with witches and fairies, which makes elder wands and staffs very well suited in fairy magic.

Elder wands could be used in ritual to invite fairy allies while keeping out non-friendly or outright ill-meaning entities.

Mark the boundaries of your ritual space by carrying an elder staff or wand while walking around and ask the Elder spirit to protect your space. Use elder wands or charms containing elder flowers and fruits in healing magic and protection charms. See Part 3 for health and protection charms that use elder.

Elm
(Ulmus campestris, U. glabra)

Elm is very popular with elves, the Norse equivalent of the Side in the Celtic languages speaking cultures. For this reason, elm is also named Elven (Cunningham, 1985, Gundarsson, 2007). Elm propitiates the presence of elves, so if you seek partnerships among them use elm in your ritual.

Have elm leaves or twigs on your altar, use an elm wand or elm staff in ritual, and add elm leaves, seeds and/or a tiny bit of bark to a pouch to wear when you seek to invite the presence of elves. You can wear an elm wood amulet to the same effect. Elm is listed in Part 3 among the ingredients in charms and tools intended to attract elves' presence and to facilitate interacting with them.

Furze/Gorse
Ulex europaeus, U. galii)

Only a few examples mention furze, or gorse, in connection with fairies but they reveal important details. Irish lore has few stories about fairies appearing in the proximity of furze bushes always in circumstances related to abundance. In one story, a farmer retrieves his cow near a furze bush where a fairy man appears. The fairy man asks the farmer not to sell the cow. The cow gives great milk from that moment on. After the incident, the man "is magically helped to retrieve a large sum of money that had been taken away from him (Mac Coitir, 2018, p.92).

Another story tells about a farmer, in debt, who encounters a ghost nearby furze growing on a mound. In Irish lore there is a strong overlap between fairies and the human dead, with some humans joining the fairies after they die. The ghost, a chieftain from long ago, helps the man not only to pay his debt but to actually become rich (Mac Coitir, 2018, p.93).

I find therefore furze suited for use in fairy magic for abundance. Use furze in rituals where you petition fairy help for solving financial problems. If there's a place in your yard that you wish to dedicate to fairy allies, (See Appendix A: Fairy Garden) you could plant some furze there.

Hawthorn
(Crategus monogyna, C. laevigata)

In Celtic languages speaking cultures, hawthorns have strong ties to fairies. Not every hawthorn is a fairy tree, but still, treating hawthorns with particular regard is always a good idea because one can never know for sure. Solitary hawthorns that grow in peculiar places, or hawthorns adjoined to fairy mounds and ancient stone circles are acknowledged as fairy trees. Folklore mentions hawthorns functioning as fairy dwellings or portals to their realms (Cunningham, 1985; Daimler, 2016).

According to Scottish lore, ash, oak, and hawthorn growing together mark places where fairies can be seen, and if someone seeks to make contact with the Fairy realm they should sleep under a lone hawthorn, on May Day eve or on the eve of Midsummer (Hopman, 2010). Some hawthorns are mentioned as clootie trees, and this could indicate the possibility of petitioning the otherworldly denizens for aid in healing. Hawthorn's dual nature and connection to fairies makes it suitable for use in both connecting with fairies and keeping away those whose presence is unwanted.

Hazel
(Corylus avellana)

The connection between hazel and fairies is rather tenuous. Irish lore mentions one incident where a man held onto a black handle knife and a hazel twig to fight off the fairies trying to abduct his wife (Mac Coitir, 2018). Generally, in Irish lore hazel is connected to wisdom. I would suggest using hazel in circumstances that warrant its need for defense against fairy attacks. Having strong allies among fairies and related god figures is the best line of defense in my opinion, and making friends is always preferable to adversarial confrontation. So use hazel only in extreme circumstances. Make sure you offer abundantly to your fairy allies to make it clear that the drastic measures are not directed at them.

Holly
(Ilex aquifolium)

Several traditions mention holly's connection to magic and fairies. In Scotland, on New Year's Eve, holly branches were brought indoors for decoration and as wards against malevolent fairies. Irish lore mentions holly as a tree that fairy favors, and misusing or abusing a holly tree would annoy fairies (Mac Coitir, 2015). Using holly in ritual facilitates communication with elves, especially Ljosalfar and land wights (Gundarsson, 2007).

Lugh, an Irish god with ties to the sidhe, has some connection to holly. Lugh has a reputation for martial skills; holly is also mentioned as a choice of wood for spears, arrows, and chariot building (Mac Coitir, 2015). This would make holly an excellent choice for fairy magic, whether defensive or offensive. In his *Encyclopedia of Magical Herbs*, Scott Cunningham mentions holly as "a par excellence protective herb" (Cunningham, 1985). I personally incorporate holly leaves and bits of wood in almost all protection charms. You can find details about how to make protective charms that include holly, in Part 3.

Juniper
(Juniperus communis)

Juniper has been used for purifying and cleansing in folk traditions across Europe from the Mediterranean to Scotland (Cunningham, 1985). In Scotland, burning juniper to purify a space with smoke is called saining. As popular belief has it, smoke that results from burning juniper cleanses stagnant energy and sends away disease-causing, and ill-meaning spirits more generally. Cattle are sained and juniper placed before them in the byre at the beginning of Easter lent to protect against harm from witches and theft by the fairies (Mac Coitir, 2015).

Juniper smoke can be used to energetically cleanse spaces and people more generally, and to protect against harm caused by fairies. If you seek to build fairy partnerships, do not use juniper liberally. Rather, strengthen your alliances among fairies including those with deities related to them as your first line of defense. If you use juniper – which works wonderfully in cleansing spaces from stagnant energy such as in the room of a sick person – communicate your intent to your fairy ally first and make abundant offerings so saining will not come across as an act of hostility. See Appendix C for a more elaborate offering-making ritual adapted from Romanian fairy tradition.

Oak
(Quercius alba, Q. rubra, Q. robur, Q. virgininana, Q. palustris, Q. macrocarpa, Q. petrea, Q. velutina, Q. lyrata)

Oak lore is very abundant and oak's ties to fairies are well-known. Oak, ash, and thorn growing together mark a place where fairies can be seen (Hopman, 2010). Welsh lore mentions fairies' affinity for female oak trees. To see fairies, one should go out on a Friday evening and sit inside a fairy ring found under a female oak tree (Sterling, 2022). Some scholars connect An Dagda, the Irish god also known as King of Fairies in Ireland, to oak trees. Lightning marks on the trunk of an oak tree are sometimes attributed to Dagda's axe. This is based on a passage from Cath Maige Tuired, where king Indech's daughter threatens to hinder An Dagda in battle by turning herself into a thick forest of oaks and blocking his way. At which An Dagda replies that he would then become the axe that fells the oaks. (Jones's Celtic Encyclopedia, https://www.maryjones.us/jce/dagda.html) Fairy lore from several Celtic language-speaking cultures recommend drawing a circle around oneself with an oak stick to protect against unwanted fairy advances (Mac Coitir, 2015).

Same as other trees that have a dual nature in regard to fairies, oak can help you invite fairy allies and An Dagda himself while simultaneously protecting against fairies that pose a threat. In Fairy Witchcraft practiced and taught by Morgan Daimler, oak is connected to the Lord of the Wildwood, one of the four main Fairy liminal gods (Daimler, 2016). If you choose to use oak wands or sticks in your practice, express clearly your intent about who you wish to invite in your ritual space and who you want to keep out.

Pear Tree
(Pyrus communis)

All across Europe, from east to west, the pear tree is known as a fairy tree. In Romania, offerings to fairies are left under certain pear trees and fairy-related rituals occur in their proximity. Pear trees feature in both living lore and tales describing Fairy (Simina, 2023). There are first-hand accounts of fairy seers going into trance near pear trees and being taken up these trees by the fairies they interact with (Vivod, 2018). Accounts from Ireland present the pear as one of the trees with ties to fairies.

As the pear tree is part of the Rosaceae family, here in Ireland it is connected to the hawthorn, rowan, wild cherry, blackthorn and crab apple. All trees with a particular association with the good people as well, you might notice. (Halpin, 2019)

A story in the Irish folklore collection available at www.duchas. ie tells about a man who takes shelter behind a pear tree to avoid being harmed by fairies. (https://www.duchas.ie/en/cbes/5008852/4961113)

As it is the case with many trees connected to fairies, the lore of pear trees recommends them for both connecting with and protecting from these beings.

You could plant a pear tree in your yard, and make it a welcoming place for your fairy allies by leaving offerings nearby. It can be a place for you to journey, meditate, journal, and connect with your fairy guides in general.

In case you cannot plant a tree, you could maybe have a twig on your altar, or a picture of a pear tree (best if this is a pear tree that you actually know.) Use a pear wand to mark the ritual space, speaking out who do you call in and who do you intend to keep out

Rowan

(Sorbus aucuparia, S. domestica, S. aria) European

Fairy lore from western Europe abounds in examples where rowan is used to protect against malicious fairies. In Ireland, Scotland, and Wales rowan branches are brought into the stalls to prevent fairies from stealing animals or inflicting diseases upon them. Equal-arms crosses made of two rowan sticks tied together with red thread is a charm against many kinds of evil including harm caused by fairies (MacCoitir, 2015). However, not all fairies are averse to rowan. Rowan berries are a favorite food for the Tuatha Dé Danann, the Irish gods who went to live among the Sidhe when Ireland was taken over by Milesians. In Scotland, the rowan berries are also known as a favorite food for fairies, "…which is why they [rowans] are often seen near stone cairns and circles in Scotland" (Hopman, 2010, p.169).

Lore recommends rowan as both a tree that fairies favor as well as one that can offer protection against harm caused by them (Daimler, 2016; MacCoitir, 2015). Rowan berries make great offerings. To avoid offending or hurting fairy allies by using iron, a rowan ritual blade is a very good substitute (Hopman, 2010). Rowan lends itself to the creation of selective protections that allow fairy allies to join while keeping out the others.

Yew

(Taxus baccata, T. brevifolia, T. Canadensis)

Yew is one of the trees with the highest longevity, and is associated with magic and fairies in various European cultures. In Norse mythology, Yggdrasil, the World Tree, is believed to be an ash tree but some argue that it might be in fact yew. Nine realms aggregate around Yggdrasil, with Alfheim, the realm of Elves, being one of them. Yggdrasil is therefore indissolubly connected to the Elves and suited for use in elf magic. Gundarsson recommends using yew when working to open the lines of communication with land wights and members of the Álfar, (the powerful Norse and Germanic elves, not the commercial version, Santa's elves) Using yew in ritual and carrying yew amulets facilitate seeing the elves as well as communicating with them (Gundarsson, 2007).

Willow

(Salix alba, S. arctica, S. amygdaloides,
S. aegyptiaca, S. caprea, S. cinerea, S. discolor)

Lore that relates willow to fairies is scant at best. *A New Dictionary of Fairies* mentions an older belief about willows walking behind travelers at night scaring them. This may connect willows to water fairies who are ambivalent and more often than not, dangerous (Daimler, 2020).

In modern styles of Fairy Witchcraft, willow is associated with the powers of the moon and water (Daimler, 2016). I was recommended willow by my fairy allies to use in charms for healing especially in situations where inflammation is present, and when dealing with emotional and psychological upheaval. More on incorporating willow into practical uses in Part 3.

Chapter 3

Resins and Tree-related Materials

Amber

(Electrum)

According to the Merriam-Webster dictionary, amber is a hard yellowish to brownish translucent fossil resin that takes a fine polish and is used chiefly in making ornamental jewelry (such as beads). (https://www.merriam-webster.com/dictionary/amber) Amber results from coniferous trees oozing sap that solidified. The age of amber deposits around the world varies largely, from approximately thirty million years to about forty thousand years. (https://www.getty.edu/publications/ambers/intro/4/)

Amber was here long before the first humans walked the Earth. I regard it as a bearer of memories from a time when nature reigned supreme, and of times when the Otherworld was more present if not more involved in earthly matters.

The link between amber and elves is rather tenuous but still worthy of consideration. Modern lore connects amber with Freya (Daimler, 2023). The tears Freya's cries over her estranged husband turn into gold when they touch the ground and into amber when they drop into water (Gundarsson, 1993). Freya owns Brísingamen, a famous magical gold necklace crafted by the Duergar. According to more modern interpretations of lore, Brisingamen was made of amber or at least included amber (Daimler 2023). Amber's golden color, its possible link to Brísingamen and relationship to Freya's tears makes it a suitable material for decorating altars dedicated to Freya.

Freya is the one who taught seiðr to the Æsir, Norse gods. Seiðr, a specific practice of magic, takes the name of Álfseiðr when it involves the elves. Álfseiðr is understood as magic practiced by elves, and/or by witches who work in partnership with elves. Knowledge of seiðr and its application as Álfseiðr becomes thus one thread among several others that relate Freya and the Álfar. Freya's brother, Freyr is lord of Álfheim, the Land of Elves. In Ynglinga Saga, Freyr, euhemerized as a king, continues to receive offerings after his death. Being buried in a mound, Freyr, or Fro Ing, relates thus to the mound elves. It is Freya, who officiating as priestess, presides over the offerings poured into the mound to maintain peace and prosperity in the land (Sturluson, 1991, Daimler, 2023; Heath, 2022).

Due to its golden color and symbolism, relationship to Freya, and indirectly to Freyr and Álfar, amber is a good choice of material for amulets, charms, offerings, and any ritual that involves the elves. I have found out that not only elves, but a broad spectrum of fairies and fairy beings like amber. Amber acts selectively, inviting fairy allies while screening out fairy beings who are not goodly inclined and energies that are not synergistic to the purpose of the ritual or magical working. In some witchcraft traditions amber, especially in combination with jet, is known to offer protection against ill-meaning spirits and many kinds of psychic attacks. A necklace or bracelet of amber and jet (discussed next) is not only a beautiful piece of jewelry but a very practical one too.

Jet

(Gagates)

Jet, also named "black amber," is in fact lignite, a coal. Like all coal, lignite derived from wood that changed its structure under enormous pressure until becoming a mineraloid. Jet formed about one hundred and fifty, to two hundred million years ago. It has been used in jewelry, art, domestic activities, and presumably healing and religious practices, since the Neolithic period.

Same as amber, jet is loosely associated with Freya, and following the same tenuous link one may connect jet to the elves (See Amber). Despite the fact that there is no explicit depiction of Freya spinning, in lore she is nonetheless connected to this activity. Flax is known as 'Freya's Hair' and the constellation Orion an 'Freya's Distaff' (Daimler, 2023; Heath, 2021). Spinning and magic are strongly related, and Freya is a goddess of magic. The Álfar have their own type of magic that very likely includes spinning. Spindle whorls made of jet, amber, or jet and amber combined have been discovered among grave goods from Bronze and Iron Ages. While not straightforward, the link between spinning, Freya, elves, and jet or amber is discernible for those who take time to read and analyze the lore.

In my experience, jet is protective against ill-meaning spirits and fairies. I find it grounding, and energetically connected with the Earth, as the Earth was a very long time ago. To the magical practitioner, jet feels friendly and somewhat lenient, meaning that charms or spells involving jet are not likely to backfire violently: this depends, of course, on the other ingredients being used and what exactly the spell or charm is about.

Jewelry made of jet and amber is protective. Used independently or together with other materials, jet – by its association with coals and therefore fire – can hallow and protect ritual spaces and those gathered within. I found that some among the elves – Dwergar or Svartalfar in particular – like jet, and the use jet propitiates their presence.

Dragon Blood
(Dracaena draco, Calamus draco, Pterocarpus)

Dragon blood is a natural plant resin. Since very old times dragon blood has been valued for its bright red pigment and used in dyeing cloth and textile fibers. It has been employed medicinally to treat various inflammatory and gastric complaints and made it into modern pharmacopeia (https://www.healthline.com/health/dragons-blood#TOC_TITLE_HDR_1) Dragon blood is widespread in spiritual practices as incense or pigment for ritual marking and painting. In Romanian fairy tradition, dragon blood is an important ingredient found in protection charms against Rusalii. The Rusalii are mercurial fairies feared for the harm they may cause to people, oftentimes for no apparent reason, but also deeply revered for their healing powers and connection with the dead (Simina, 2023). In rural areas, once per year, groups of men gather to dance the ritual dance of Cālusari, a practice believed to be thousands of years old. The dancers, organized similarly to ancient warrior bands, act under the protection of Rusalia, the Queen of Rusalii. On this special occasion, the Cālusari receive permission from the Queen herself to heal ailments caused by fairies (Eliade, 1973; Kligman, 1981). During performance, dancers carry pouches filled with various herbs, dragon blood among those, which they give or sell to people gathered to watch. It is also customary for women to try to steal threads from the Cālusari's belts and bits of the herbs they carry, because being worn during the ritual these samples have acquired amplified powers to heal and protect (Kligman, 1981; Simina, 2023).

I personally use dragon blood in protective magic and/ or to amplify the strength of other ingredients. I find that incorporating dragon blood gives spells a certain 'bite' and fiery quality that I like. My allies and familiars, who are primarily from among the Álfar, do not object to dragon blood, and actually recommended that I use it in manifestation magic as well, by sprinkling some powdered resin over things that I am about to burn. Probably it would be wise for you to check in with your own fairy allies and familiars before incorporating dragon blood in ritual work.

Frankincense
(Boswellia sacra, B. carterii)

Frankincense is an aromatic resin used in making incense and is added to fragrant oils for cosmetic or ritual purpose. Frankincense has been used for millennia in religious and spiritual practices: frankincense, plain or mixed with other ingredients, is burned to hallow spaces and drive out ill-meaning spirits, troublesome dead, and malicious demons. Largely, Christianity's view of fairies as demonic beings led to burning frankincense (along with the use of Christian symbols and prayers) to keep them away.

Frankincense has always been a precious commodity, regarded as a gift suitable for kings and gods. In ancient Egypt, frankincense was burned at sunrise to honor Ra, the Sun God (Cunningham, 1985). Christian tradition mentions several instances of frankincense and myrrh in conjunction with high status biblical figures.[8] Frankincense was on par with gold, not only because of its rarity and beautiful fragrance but also due to its practical use as an antimicrobial. At a time when antibiotics were unknown, frankincense's antiseptic properties justified its exorbitant price (https://www.ncbi.nlm.nih.gov/pmc/articles/PMC9268443/). In the act of sympathetic magic, the spirit energy of frankincense would annihilate the spirit of disease in the same way as its chemical compounds would kill the disease causing germs.

Frankincense makes a great offering to the Álfar, and to all fairy beings that are hæl and holy. Quoting Cat Heath, "...hæl[9] and holy plants aren't inimical to hæl and holy beings." I truly believe this to always be the case.

Petrified Wood

Petrified wood is not actually wood, yet has strong ties to trees and to a remote geological past. About three hundred million years ago, when dinosaurs roamed the Earth and plants grew gigantic, trees fell and sunk into minerals-saturated, muddy waters. In the absence of oxygen, decomposition slowed down dramatically while permineralization – the process by which minerals permeate all the cells in the fallen, sunken trees –

occurred. Permineralization continued until all cellulose had been replaced with mineral deposits. The cell walls in the tree trunk initially provided a template for the minerals to be deposited. Then, when the cellulose walls finally broke down, a magnificent replica of stone (mineral deposits) had replaced the original tree. The tree itself, both is and isn't. Its shape, memory, and energy still live encapsulated in the rocky mold while the wood itself has vanished.

I see petrified wood as the epitome of a liminal state or space: the tree connects the ancient past and the present through its metamorphosis from something transient such a tree into something immortal, namely stone. For me, a petrified tree is a metaphor for an Otherworldly process by which beings transform and acquire bodies that live forever.

I find petrified wood to be a great journey companion whenever I seek to make a connection with spiritual ancestors. Its presence in the ritual space is an anchor into times that are beyond the memory of bloodlines and a portal that enables elven, fairy, and wight spiritual ancestors, teachers, and the oldest of guides, to join.

I use petrified wood in energetic healing and healing magic to speed up bone recovery from fractures, deficient mineral absorption, osteoporosis, etc. I emphasize that energetic, spiritual, and magic done for health and healing is NOT a substitute for medical care but a valuable aid in making conventional cures work faster, better, and shorten recovery time. This is all personal gnosis, so check for yourself and see how you and your fairy allies resonate with petrified wood.

Chapter 4

Herbs and Flowers

Basil

(Ocimum basilicum)

In Abrahamic religions – and monotheistic religions in general – basil is one of the main herbs employed in religious ritual and ceremony (https://botanica.ugr.es/pages/publicaciones/separatas/2019_Econ_Bot/%21). In Romania, a strongly Christian country, basil is the best known and most widespread herb that everyone uses. Priests use a bunch of dried basil dipped in holy water to bless the congregation during mass, to ritually cleanse and bless houses during specific holidays, or to bless couples as part of the wedding ceremony. Basil is involved in making holy water and to bless the water in the baptismal font. When priests are called in to perform exorcism on a person, a house, or a specific space in a household, they use basil to asperse, in addition to burning incense and reciting prayers.

Medicine women and fairy seers also use basil to protect against malevolent fairies and spirits. In the footage recorded in Eastern Serbia by Dr. Maria Vivod, the viewer can see Ivanka, the fairy seer, holding a sprig of basil while dancing in a trance. (https://www.youtube.com/watch?v=ekXf7Z8G21o)

In her book *Călus: Symbolic Transformation in Romanian Ritual*, Dr. Kligman details the use of basil as part of a ritual performance intended not only to protect against but also reverse harm done by Rusalii, the very dangerous fairy beings.

I saw my own grandmother using basil for protection, hallowing spaces, folk healing, and all kinds of magic. Grandma never saw a sharp dichotomy between her own Christian beliefs and fairy beliefs, and her spiritual practice was a syncretic blend of both.

I rarely use basil, but I can suggest it for hallowing spaces and purification rituals where dried basil could be used for both aspersing and smoke cleansing. I would also recommend it for planting around the house to keep away negative energy, and malevolent spirits. Dried basil can be worn alone or in combination with apotropaic herbs to escape unwanted fairy attention. More on basil and other apotropaic herbs in Part 3.

Clover, Four Leaf
(Trifolium)

A four-leaf clover is an anomaly occurring in the three-leaf clover. The chance to find a four-leaf clover among regular three-leaf clovers is one in ten thousand. Because of the rarity, finding one four-leaf clover is believed to signal good luck. In Irish lore, a four-leaf clover is known to break glamor, an ability that fairies have to hide things in plain sight or make them look like something else. Carrying a four-leaf clover breaks fairy enchantment and helps one see fairies (MacCoitir, 2015). Caveat on his last one: spying is never a good idea. Fairies hate intruders as much as humans hate violation of their privacy. Use common sense in employing a four-leaf clover and any herb with similar properties to the purpose of fairy seeing. If you only seek to satisfy a mere curiosity, then better not pursue it. If, however, you believe you need an aid to see fairies in order to communicate better with your fairy allies, then announce your intentions and ask for their help, make offerings, ask for permission, and proceed, only if allowed.

Cowslip
(Primula veris)

Cowslip has a fairy association in several European cultures. Known by the popular name of 'key flower', 'key herb', or 'fairy cups', cowslip, in combination with other herbs, is said to have the power to open the gates to the Otherworld (Gundarsson,

2007). In Romania, this is one of the flowers that fairies favor and which they bless in their passing on May Eve and the eve of Midsummer.

Cowslip is pleasant to fairies and invites the presence of the goodly inclined ones while offering protection against other less benevolent beings. Bundles of cowslip can decorate the altar, ritual space, and the house during May Day (Bealtaine, Walpurgisnacht) and Midsummer holidays. Used in fairy magic, cowslip preserves youthfulness, it promotes victory over adversity, and brings abundance.

Early Purple Orchid
(Orchis mascula)

In Roman mythology, early purple orchids were known as food for satyrs, fairy-like beings (MacCoitir, 2015). In Greek mythology, Orchis, the son of a satyr and a nymph, was turned into a flower upon his death (https://depts.washington.edu/popctr/orchids.htm). In ancient Greek, orkis means testicle, and the plant itself was considered an aphrodisiac. In Irish and Scottish folk magic, the early purple orchid is known for use in spells to attract a male partner. The male specific association is due to the orchid bulbs resembling testicles (Hopman, 2010). We find the early purple orchid listed among ingredients for a charm against unwanted attention from "…persistently affectionate elfs…." (Gundarsson, 2007).

A mix of dried early purple orchid, cowslip, elder blossoms, and mugwort help open the gates to the Otherworld (Gundarsson, 2007). Sprinkle the mixture around yourself and on the altar during ritual, or wear a pouch containing these herbs to facilitate communicating with elves and possibly other fairies.

The information seems somewhat contradictory. Early purple orchid appears in charms to elicit sexual attraction, is connected to satyrs and in at least one case with nymphs which makes the erotic connotations all the more obvious, opens gates to otherworld, but it is also recommended to stall unwanted advances from elves and similar beings.

If you wish to incorporate early purple orchids in your rituals and charms, I would suggest learning as much as you possibly can about the lore surrounding the fairy beings you are connected to and find out as much as you can about their likes and dislikes. Ask your fairy allies about the appropriateness of using orchids. The last thing you want is to chase away your allies and attract the advances of those whom you seek you keep at bay.

Elecampane
(Inula helenium)

Elecampane is called elf-doc in Denmark, elf-doc or elf-herb in England.

> *...and elecampane is so closely tied to the elfs that thrusting a knife into an elecampane plant is the key element in one Anglo-Saxon charm against alf-caused illness.* (Gundarsson 2007)

When I lived in Italy, I learned that elecampane is called *herba degli elfi,* meaning elf-herb or elfwort. I also learned that sprinkling around powdered elecampane attracts fairies. It would be a logical conclusion that having elecampane growing in the area where a ritual is held invites the presence of fairy beings. I am not a great fan of cutting fresh flowers of any kind for bouquets; I am concerned about hindering seed spreading and thus endangering survival of annual plants. So, I made a satchel with a few dried flower heads which I put on my altar or have with me in ritual. I have had the satchel for several years and I prefer using this to cutting fresh flowers every time. I also want to try planting elecampane in a particular space in my yard as an offering to my allies among fairy beings.

Fern
(Polydopodiopsida)

In Scottish lore, ferns are believed to grow abundantly on cairns where fairies live, usually to camouflage the entrance.

> *On Samhuinn night the ferry-kairds (ferns) are seen to part as the Peerie-folk emerge on their travels.* (Hopman, 2010)

I would take the presence of fern growing in unusual places as a possible clue for a fairy entrance, and consequently I would mark that as a place to either avoid entirely or leave offerings nearby. In any case, a fairy entrance and any kind of fairy spot or tree should be treated with respect and left undisturbed. If you must plant or build and have no way to spare the fern and the entrance it shelters, talk with the fairies living there, explain clearly and politely what is about to happen, leave offerings, and also offer an alternative location for them to move. Take omens to check about how to proceed because it may take some negotiation. The European fairy lore abounds in examples of people disrespecting fairy presence and damaging plants or places associated with them. The consequences are usually disastrous for the humans involved. If you seek to build connections with fairies, no matter what type or cultural provenance, and if you wish to make allies among them, damaging anything of theirs' will work against your intent.

Foxglove
(Digitalis purpurea)

Foxglove is also known by many folk names, fairy fingers, fairy petticoats, fairy thimbles, fairy weed, all suggesting this plant's connection to fairies (Cunningham, 1985). In the lore of Celtic speaking cultures, foxglove is a symbol of the beauty and power of the Otherworld. Foxglove is known as a plant that fairies themselves favor, so wearing it or having it grow around invites fairy presence. Foxglove is used medicinally in minute doses, but it is lethal in large amounts. In folk medicine foxglove is used in treating painful spots caused by elf-shot. Foxglove would also work well on people under fairy spells (MacCoitir, 2015).

Both Irish and Romanian folk medicine practitioners recommend harvesting foxglove on Midsummer because at that time fairies fly around and while passing, they bless different herbs (Simina, 2023; Ghinoiu, 2020).

Foxglove makes a nice and magical addition to gardens by inviting fairy presence but also offering means to protect against fairy-induced diseases. To avoid constant cutting and eventually damaging foxglove plants, you can dry a sprig and keep it on the altar, or make a satchel with few dried flower heads.

Garlic

(Allium sativum)

Garlic is known almost universally in European folk magic as repellent for any kind of malevolent entities from among ghosts, demons, or fairies. Whether the repelling qualities are due to its strong odor, high sulfur content, or the combination of these, garlic is one of the strongest defense herbs to employ in case of sustained attacks from ill-meaning beings and spirits. Romanian folk traditions recommend wearing garlic in protective amulets and charms and hanging garlic braids around windows and above doors around specific times of the year when dangerous fairies roam around (Simina, 2023; Ghinoiu, 2020; Kligman, 1981). Italian folk tradition of Sicily recommends garlic harvested before sunrise as a talisman against evil magic and evil spirits of any kind.

I don't use garlic except for cooking; I don't have any prohibition about using it, it's more of a visceral feeling that I get around garlic, if I am to bring it in a ritual space. I would suggest checking first with your fairy allies, if garlic is something you can use. Just in case.

Hollyhock
(Alcea rosea)

Aside from illustrations that became popular during the Victorian era, illustrations which show little fairies wearing dresses made of hollyhock flowers, information about fairies' connection to this plant is almost non-existing. And no, I don't believe that any fairy would wear clothing items made of hollyhock. However, my own grandmother, a medicine woman and fairy seer, planted a lot of hollyhocks in our yard. I have multiple reasons to believe that Grandma planted those flowers not only for their beauty but also as a token for the fairies she worked in partnership with.

My personal gnosis is that fairies do favor hollyhocks (albeit not wearing the flowers as clothing). In support of this, I found hollyhock mentioned in a charm for seeing fairies dating from the seventeenth century (Starza, 2023). I caution against spying on fairies, but if you need any aid to improve your ability to communicate with your allies, hollyhock could help. As always, consult with your fairy allies and use common sense.

Lady Bedstraw and Yellow Bedstraw
(Galium verum; Cruciata laeviceps)

Fairy traditions from both Romania and Ireland record lady bedstraw and yellow bedstraw as herbs related to fairies. In Romanian lore this connection is straight forward. Both varieties, lady bedstraw (*Galium verum*) and yellow bedstraw (*Cruciata laevipes*) are known under the name sânziene, and are sacred to the eponymous fairies. Sânziene, the fairies, are typically benevolent toward humans. Love magic, fertility, and herbal healing are all within Sânziene's purview. On their holiday, the Feast of Sânziene, celebrated on Midsummer, people gather bunches of sânziene (flowers) to hang on gates and bring inside their homes to invite the blessings of Sânziene (fairies) and ward off malicious entities. People wear sânziene garlands and wreaths which they later use for love divination.

The most famous fairy witch in Ireland, Biddy Early, recommended on at least one occasion the use of a plant known as Lady's fingers as a remedy to fairy-induced disease. Lady's fingers[10] has been identified as lady's bedstraw, *(Galium verum)*, (Lenihan, 1987). Whatever the folk name, lady's bedstraw, lady's fingers, or sânziene, this herb is known for its close ties to fairies in both Irish and Romanian traditions.

Bringing lady's bedstraw in the ritual space invites the presence of fairies. At Midsummer, you may have a few flowers on the altar as an offering to fairies. You may add dried lady's bedstraw to your witch pouch if you have one, or included in charms and amulets destined to draw fairies closer to you and facilitate communication.

Lavender
(Lavandula)

Lavender is deeply relaxing, which makes it a valuable aid in attaining meditative altered states of consciousness which facilitate communication with fairy allies. Lavender is also known by the name of elf leaf which suggests an affinity that elves have for this plant. In my experience, lavender is favored by many kinds of fairies, not just elves. I am fond of lavender because it was one of the first herbs I became acquainted with for magical purposes. My grandmother grew lavender in our yard, and I used to help her make bundles which we would then hang to dry. As a fairy witch I use lavender for almost everything: healing magic, hallowing space in preparation for ritual, and in offerings to deity and fairy guides. It is a forgiving and very versatile herb. Using lavender by mistake as the "wrong" ingredient in a spell or ritual would probably go unnoticed given lavender's versatility and easy going nature. In Part 3, you will find lavender involved in almost every kind of charm, spell, or ritual.

Leek

(Alllium porrum)

In Norse lore, leek is connected to Freyr. Since Freyr is ruler of Alfheim, leeks are by association an herb favored by the Álfar. Freyr is related to fertility and fertility magic. In ritual, leaks can be used to asperse water to hallow a space (Paxon, 2021). Leeks can be used as ingredients in any fertility spell or charm especially when calling upon Freyr, Freya, mound elves, and land wights to help. Dishes that include leeks make good offerings to elves and land wights (and to fairies in general).

Mugwort

(Artemisia vulgaris)

Mugwort is among the best known apotropaics. In Romania, mugwort is heavily relied upon to defend against Iele, the unfriendly fairies, and against demons and ghosts seeking to cause damage. (Kligman, 1981; Pócs, 1989). Norse traditions mention mugwort as protective against potentially dangerous elves but also as means to enhance communication with some of the Álfar (Gundarsson, 2007). Rubbed onto ritual tools such as wands, staffs, runes (or other tools used for divination) mugwort amplifies their powers. To enhance sight and hearing therefore enhancing the ability to communicate with elves (and fairies in general), rub mugwort onto tools and charms that you wish to consecrate for this purpose. You can also pass your tools, charms, and amulets through mugwort smoke in addition or instead of rubbing them with the herb. Along with your clearly formulated intentions, mugwort will repel unfriendly beings and facilitate the connection with friendly ones.

Primrose

(Primula vulgaris)

Primroses are among those flowers that fairies favor (Cunningham, 1985). In Romanian lore, primroses are linked to fairies in the same way as the sânziene and cowslip are. (See the entries for Cowslip, and Lady's Bedstraw.) Primrose, *Primula vulgaris,* and cowslip, *Primula veris,* are very closely related and can be used as substitutes for one another in ritual. Having primroses grow unexpectedly in one's backyard could indicate fairies' preference for that spot. That may become a space to leave offerings and honor fairy allies. As it is always the case with places that fairies claim for themselves, do not disturb it. If interfering with that spot is unavoidable, talk first with the fairies who claimed it, offer hospitality in another location, and act accordingly to the feedback you receive. Primroses brought into ritual space, placed on the altar, or carried in a pouch will attract fairy presence and facilitate communication with fairy allies.

Rose

(Rosa rubiginosa)

There are many references about roses' connection to fairies and the use of roses in fairy witchcraft. Planted in the garden, roses attract fairies (Cunningham, 1985). In Romania, roses are sacred to the Rusalii, mercurial fairies, also known as Iele. The name of the fairy queen, Rusalia or Rosalia, derives from *rosa,* the Latin for rose. The feast of Rusalii and the pre-Christian tradition of ancestor veneration have been absorbed into Christianity and linked to Pentecost. On this day roses are brought to graveyards, and offerings of food and pottery are made for the deceased. Throughout the week that precedes the holiday of Rusalii, places connected to these fairies are to be avoided, and in some areas of the country it is part of tradition to leave out offerings for them. Rusalii have associations with the dead; roses are brought to the graveyards not only for the ancestors but also for the Rusalii as means to acknowledge them (Simina, 2023; Kligman, 1981).

In Fairy Witchcraft, as practiced and taught by Morgan Daimler, roses are used for gentle cleansing, energizing, and the thorny stalks for protection magic and cursing (Daimler, 2016). Roses are among the flowers that I use most often in my personal practice. I put a few drops of rose oil in the water that I sprinkle when hallowing the grounds in preparation for ritual to make the space more inviting for my fairy allies and the Liminal Powers that I might call upon. In spiritual healing, I use the energy of rose thorns to "burst" open clusters of stagnant energy to allow it to drain. I find this approach particularly useful in situations where pent-up emotions are part of the problem. I find that the energy of rose petals – brought in through a few dried petals that I keep in a satchel or as a drop of rose oil which I rub on my hands – is soothing, calming, relaxing, and helpful in situations where there's a need for finding closure. (This is NOT a substitute for working with a qualified therapist and going to counseling. Any form of spiritual healing should be used to support conventional forms of intervention, not as a replacement.)

Rosemary
(Salvia Rosmarinus / Rosmarinus officinalis)

Known by the folk name 'elf leaf', rosemary attracts the presence of elves (Cunningham, 1985). In Romanian folklore, rosemary is known for both its protective qualities and use in love magic. Growing rosemary in the garden will render the place pleasant to fairy beings (Cunningham, 1985). Dried rosemary can be burned or sprinkled around, and fresh rosemary twigs can be used to asperse water to hallow a place for ritual. For cleansing diseased energy and banishing malevolent fairies and spirits, burn dried rosemary either by itself or in combination with mugwort.

Sage
(Salvia officinalis, S. apiana)

As the name shows, common sage, *Salvia officinalis,* white sage, *Salvia apiana,* and *Salvia Rosmarinus,* are related. Being all members of the genus *Salvia,* common sage, white sage and rosemary share many energetic and magical properties. Similar to rosemary, sage is used to purify ritual spaces. And also similarly to rosemary, sage can be burned as an offering to fairy allies and other Powers that you to honor. These similarities and the possibility of interchangeable use begs the question, which one to use and when.

When choosing, here are several aspects to consider. Both sage and rosemary are used in cooking worldwide so you don't need to take a trip to any metaphysical store nor order anything expensive online. What you need in your ritual may be right inside your pantry. You may favor herbs that are indigenous to the area you live in; this is especially relevant if the fairy beings that you work with are also native to the area.

However, your fairy allies may be from a culture that is different from the area where you currently live. For example, I am native to Romania, I live in the United States, and my path is Álfatru, Norse elven magic with a tinge of Irish paganism. Most of my fairy allies and familiars are Norse-Gaelic, which means that I am straddling Irish and Icelandic/Germanic traditions.

With all this being said, I personally prefer the variety of sage *Salvia officinalis* because it is related to the land and the cultures my fairy guides originated from. However, in a pinch I will use *Salvia apiana,* the white sage. White sage is native to the United States which is where I live. It is very closely related to common sage and similar in so many ways, so it is a good substitute. When sage is not an option, I turn to rosemary that meets all the criteria.

St John's Wort
(Hypericum perforatum)

In his books of Norse paganism, Kveldulf Gundarsson calls St. John's Wort by the name Sunnawort. Sunna refers to the sun itself. As the name suggests this herb has strong solar associations. Sunnawort is favored by Ljosalfar, the Light Elves, in particular and it gives protection against darker and more dangerous beings (Gundarsson, 2007). In Ireland, St. John's Wort is known to repel fairies thus being used to protect against unwanted attention from the sidhe (Daimler, 2022). In Romania, on Midsummer Eve, the night of June 23, fairies fly or walk over fields and bless herbs for medicinal uses and magic. People gather St. John's Wort on the morning of June 24, when it is said the herb is at the peak of its power due to fairies blessing it the night before.

Since my own fairy familiars are not repelled by Sunnawort, I employ it to add an extra layer of protection when I open portals. Sprinkled throughout the space where I intend to open the portal, Sunnawort, used by itself or in combination with mugwort, creates a very strong barrier that selectively allows into the space only those allies and guides that I trust.

Vervain
(Verbena)

Since antiquity, vervain has been known as one of the most sacred and magically powerful herbs (Cunningham, 1985). In Ireland, vervain was one of the main remedies used by fairy doctors to cure diseases inflicted by fairies. Vervain is still considered one of the herbs that "nothing natural or supernatural could injure" (Mac Coitir 2015). People thus carry vervain as protection against disease, accidents, and harm caused by inimical fairy beings. Alongside mugwort and St. John's Wort, vervain features in Midsummer celebrations across Europe.

On St. John's Eve in Germany there were celebrations and bonfires were lit. People wore chaplets of vervain and mugwort for good luck. As people left the festivities they would take off the chaplet and throw it in the fire saying: 'May all my ill-luck depart and be burnt with these. In England Garlands of Vervain were worn on St. John's Day, and in France Vervain was collected before St. John's Eve and purified in the smoke of the bonfires on the feast day. (Mac Coitir, 2015)

Midsummer is widely known as a time when fairies are very active, traveling and also mingling with people. Vervain is almost omnipresent in midsummer celebrations. The existing folklore recommends vervain as a protection against malevolent entities including fairies, but also as a healing herb blessed by fairies who, in their passing, bless herbs and imbue them with power on the Midsummer Eve. Vervain is one of my go-to herbs. My allies among elves and other fairy beings I work in partnership with advised that I use vervain for both protection and in energetic healing.

Violets
(Viola)

Old lore connecting violets to fairies is sparse at best. Despite this, I included violets for discussion here given the gnosis, both my own and of other people that I know, that connects violets and fairies. In Greek myth, Proserpine and her entourage of nymphs[11] used to gather violets and other spring flowers. Proserpine appears thus related to spring and flowers, in the same way as the nymphs accompanying her are. It was during flower picking that Hades kidnapped Proserpine. In England, in popular belief, violets were linked to sadness and death (Mac Coitir, 2015). In English lore, as well as in Scottish, Welsh, and Irish lore, there is a significant overlap between fairies and the human dead. Albeit tenuous, a connection between fairies, the human dead, and violets is discernible.

I was told once by my grandmother that fairies like violets. She had in mind specifically wild violets, *Viola odorata*. Many years later, my mother shared with me her own gnosis about fairies and violets. In recent years I had quite a few experiences involving fairies, the human dead, and violets which led me to conclude that the plants in the genus Viola in general are attractive to fairies, especially to those among fairies who have contingencies to the human dead.

I see thus garden pansies, *Viola tricolor,* and all kinds of violets well suited for altars and spaces dedicated to ancestors who are in some ways connected to fairies. When violets appear in my backyard in completely unexpected locations, I take that as an indication of fairy-related spiritual ancestors being around. I suggest that you talk to your own fairy allies, inquire, and experiment to find out what holds true for you about violets and fairies.

Wormwood
(Artemisia absinthium, A. annua)
Wormwood is very closely related to mugwort, both plants being members of the *Artemisia* family. While their application in herbal medicine may be different, their esoteric qualities are very similar. Mugwort and wormwood can substitute one another in charms and protection magic. See Mugwort, discussed above.

Yarrow
(Achillea milefollium)
Yarrow is known from ancient times as a most potent herb extremely versatile in its uses. Achilles, the legendary Greek warrior is said to have used yarrow to heal his wounded

soldiers, and the very name Achillea is eponymous to him. As Greek mythology has it, Achilles was a disciple of Chiron, the wisest among Centaurs (Mac Coitir, 2015). The myths credit thus an Otherworldly source for Achilles' herbal knowledge.

Yarrow bolsters courage and draws love and true friends toward the person carrying it (Cunningham, 1985). In Ireland, yarrow for medicinal purposes was collected on Midsummer Eve, a time that is both magical and strongly associated with fairy presence. Same as vervain, yarrow is one among seven herbs whose powers cannot be overcome by anything either natural or supernatural. Depending on what forces are called upon while collecting yarrow, the herb can be used for good or evil, with equal success (Mac Coitir, 2015). An Irish charm for protection calls for collecting ten yarrow leaves: one leaf is given to the fairies, and nine are worn as a talisman (Wilde, 1991).

Norse lore mentions yarrow in conjunction with galdr (magic that involves chanting spells, incantations, etc.) and also connects yarrow to elves. (Gundarsson, 2007) In Ireland yarrow was used to protect cows and their calves from fairy-caused illness and abduction by fairies (Mac Coitir, 2015).

Yarrow is among my favorite herbs to use in magic. Like many other plants discussed here, yarrow allows the presence of fairy allies and familiars while protecting against ill-meaning fairies, spirits, and malevolent witchcraft. In Part 3, you will find yarrow among ingredients for many charms and rituals.

Chapter 5

Water

While many modern books give a lot of consideration to herbal ingredients, the water that is used together with these herbs is almost always overlooked. Yet water is ever present in magic and in fairy-related practices. Herb-infused water can be used to hollow spaces or to ritually bless people and objects. Biddy Early dispensed cures from the bottle the fairy gifted to her. Some stories specify that some of the remedies Biddy would give out were in liquid form (Lenihan, 1987). This suggests that water might have been an ingredient in her cures.

It is beyond the scope of this book to give a generic description of how water is used in magic. Instead, I will focus on water as it relates to fairy magic and fairy herbs. What follows is an overview of different "types" of water and suggestions for use in combination with fairy herbs. Please note that pairing water with different herbs and purposes as it is presented here, is very much based on my own gnosis and that of my grandmother's, and on bits of folklore that I learned over time.

I wish and hope that readers will get ideas on how to fine-tune herbal ingredients and the water they use so that the synergy between the two combined with the skill of the practitioner will yield the best possible outcome.

Dew

Lore from several cultures across Europe talk about times of the year when dew is imbued with special properties. Two such moments are May Day and Midsummer. On the nights preceding May Day and Midsummer fairies are known to be very active, flying over fields, or mingling with people.

Romanian lore tells how on these nights, fairies bless not just wild herbs used in magic and healing but also fields, gardens, and orchards. Dew preserves the magical powers of the blessings that fairies bestowed the night before. As a child I was told to walk barefoot on dewy grass and wash my face with dew on May Day and Midsummer mornings for health, beauty, good luck, and protection against malevolent spirits. Later in life I made the habit of leaving out overnight my wands and other items that I use in my practice, so they would soak in the dew that fell through the nights of May Eve and Midsummer Eve. I leave offerings when I set my things out, and respectfully ask for the blessings of the passing fairies and my own allies.

Water from Snow and Ice

Grandma loved to use water from melted snow. She said that it was good particularly for charms and cures related to youthfulness and health. Through my own experiments, I found out that snow water gives a certain oomph to spells by boosting the power of herbal ingredients. Some of my fairy allies appreciate when I asperse snow water around the altar in preparation for ritual. However, I live currently in the Southern US, and snow is extremely rare around here. The occasions that I have to collect snow are scarce. As much as I wish I could use it regularly, I only rarely have snow water for my work.

Faced with snow scarcity I thought that the next best thing would be to collect hail and use the resulting water. However, there was a noticeable difference. The water coming from the soft and white fluff blanketing the ground and coming from the ice pellets hitting the earth like bullets don't feel the same from an energetic perspective. Water coming from hail pellets lends itself well to work aimed at producing sudden change and disrupting existing patterns. Change of this nature is never smooth, and even if it holds great promise for the future it may be really difficult to deal with as it happens. If you chose to use water from hail or sleet, just give it thorough consideration and consult your fairy guides and familiars before proceeding. And if you have snow, gather it and save the water for future magic.

Rainwater

Using rainwater in magical work is a rather modern practice. At least I am personally not aware of any old lore indicating rainwater in magic or healing. Which does not mean that I don't use rain water; quite the opposite. I like to adapt old material to what is suited for me today, a modern practitioner of fairy magic, rather than replicating spells or rituals that I feel no connection with just because this is how things were done in the old times. Those old practices had been at some point brand new and probably those who introduced them ruffled many feathers among those supporting what was known from even older times. So. I use rain water, modern as this practice may be and not connected with anything ancient as it may appear.

The first use that I have for rain water is space cleansing. I think of the power that rain has to wash off dirt. I think of heavy rains, torrents, and swelled creeks carrying away all they encounter. The power of falling rain is something to be reckoned with, and each little raindrop is brimming with that energy. For space cleansing, whether it is the space where I regularly conduct energy healing sessions or any space that feels energetically dense and unwelcoming, I have a 16-ounce spray bottle containing rain water infused with herbs. (In Part 3, we will discuss cleansing with herbs and rainwater.)

The other use I have for rainwater is manifestation. Consider how rain makes vegetation grow. As I add rainwater to the other spell ingredients, I envision that which I seek to manifest growing into a mighty tree. I see the roots soaking in the rainwater that I pour, and the nutrients sympathetically represented by fairy herbs and the fairy energy called in for this work.

If this is something that resonates with you, then you have yet another way to include rainwater in your practice.

Ocean Water

Many kinds of fairies are not fond of ocean water. There are accounts of people who escape their fairy pursuers by getting into boats and off into the sea. On the other hand, the ocean is known to be home to various kinds of fairy beings. So, depending on who your fairy allies are and what you seek to accomplish, ocean water can have a place in your practice, or as in my case, not so much.

If your spiritual path is closely connected to the ocean, and if you have guides among ocean-dwelling fairies such as Manannán Mac Lir, then ocean water would be very appropriate to use in your ritual space and keep on your altar. The same holds true if your allies are from fairies connected to salt mines. Salt and ocean water will make the space all the more welcoming for them.

Ocean water has elevated salt content, and in general salt is considered apotropaic. Salt is among the things employed to escape unwanted attention from fairies, ghosts, and baneful spirits. Salt also helps to break baneful magic. To ward a space, salt can be used in combination with herbs and sometimes iron. However, if you are seeking to build partnerships among the fairies who do not belong to the ocean realm and are not connected to the underground salt deposits, then heavy use of iron and salt is very likely to undermine your efforts.

I rarely use ocean water, except in rituals to honor fairy queens and kings of the ocean. In case of possession by a malevolent spirit, ocean water can be used to wash the person (wiping the body with a cloth soaked in seawater will suffice) followed by smoke cleansing with a mix of mugwort, vervain, and St. John's Wort. If you are not trained, do not attempt to solve possession cases by yourself. And if you are trained, then you know that it is recommended to have at least one other person working alongside you.

Whatever your plans are for using ocean water, ask your guides and fairy familiars whether this is something you should do.

Water from Sacred Springs and Wells

Most if not all holy wells and springs now found under patronage of saints were once dedicated to deities and fairy monarchs. The fairy and deity associations persist, overlapping with the saints. Many wells in Ireland that are dedicated to Brigid reconcile the goddess and the saint with both aspects being honored at the same sacred wells. Lough Gur, a lake in County Limerick, Ireland is the territory of Áine, honored as both goddess and fairy queen. In the Ballad of Tam Lin, the fairy protagonist, Tam Lin, is the assigned guardian of a fountain.

I have on my altar a bottle with water from one of the wells near the Hill of Tara in County Meath, Ireland. I use the water sparsely because I never know when I'd be able to go back and refill it. Irish mythology connects Tara to An Dagda, a powerful god also known as king of all fairies in Ireland. The Hill of Tara is one of my favorite places, and I would never miss an opportunity to visit. There is a deep sense of connection, of settling, both quiet and exhilarating which overtakes me whenever I sit down by the well. When I touch the water in the bottle on my altar I feel the energy of the well of the whole place present, participating in whatever I do.

Water from wells and springs that are known for having connections to fairies funnel that energy into the work. However, you don't have to travel to exotic locations or to world-famous sites to get water from a spring that has fairy lore associated with it. If you hike and encounter a spot by a body of water where you recognize the fairy energetic signature, make an offering, ask for permission, and take some water with you. Do NOT drink from creeks, rivers, or lakes, unless you are absolutely sure it is safe to do so. You risk ingesting bacteria or chemicals. If the water has a dubious color or smell, do not touch it!

Holy Water

It took me a while to get used to the name holy water dissociated from its Christian connotations. According to the *Encyclopedia Britannica*:

> *In Christianity, holy water is water that has been specially blessed by a member of the clergy and it is used in baptism and to bless individuals, churches, homes and articles of devotion.*

My reluctance around holy water came from learning how the elves deserted the land when priests blessed land features with Christian prayers and holy water at the time when Christianity spread to Iceland. However, I also learned from my grandmother that everyone can bless water and even though it isn't considered 'holy' by the Church's standards, it is nonetheless rendered holy by whoever blessed it and the Powers called upon. Grandma and I would call it blessed water to differentiate from the holy water consecrated in church. As a side note, my grandmother was a practicing Christian as much as she was a medicine woman and a fairy seer, and never saw any conflict between the beliefs she held. So she used with equal enthusiasm both Church-made holy water and blessed water made by ourselves with fairy assistance.

Depending who are your fairy allies and what are your personal beliefs you can use water consecrated by any clergy that upholds the same spiritual path as yourself, or water that you bless by yourself or together with others participating in the ritual.

Part 3

Fairy Herbs and Fairy Magic in Practice

Chapter 1

Harvesting and Harnessing Plant Energy

If you need the physical parts of the plant, take as little as possible. A leaf or a petal are enough to add to a charm. You only need to connect with the energy, and in such a case a tiny fragment is enough. Rely as much as you can on parts that you find fallen on the ground. A small chip of bark flaked off a fallen branch is enough to bring the energy of that specific tree into your charm or ritual. By no means and for no reason whatsoever take any part, no matter how small, from specimens among protected species. It will not make your charm more potent, nor will it make you a more "special" fairy witch: instead, your action would only jeopardize the survival of an already struggling being – yes, remember that plants are beings – and with it, the entire species it belongs to. This will certainly not gain you any favors from the fairies and guardians of that place.

Harvesting is not always necessary, and in general you only need minute amounts of plant material. As previously mentioned, what you seek is the energy, not the amount of plant material. Using water is one simple way to gather all the energy that you wish without negatively impacting the plant. To do this, first ask the plant for permission, and explain that you only wish for them to lend their energy to your potions, charms, spells etc. Promise offerings in form of water, fertilizer, service etc., whatever is best suited for the situation and the plant you are talking to.

Once consent is obtained, prepare a wide-mouth jar filled with water. First, make offerings to the plant, to the spirits of the place, and to your own fairy allies (this could be as simple as pouring out fresh water and leaving out some fruit and/or a bit of bread). Then place the jar as close as possible to the plant. Ideally some twigs, leaves, stems, or flowers should hang over the water in the recipient. Read the section about water to help you decide what kind of water you should use. You may time your action with the full moon for added oomph. Leave the water in place for approximately 24 hours. Personally, I prefer to begin this ritual around noon, as the sun ascends toward its highest position, and close it the next day around the same time. In the 24 hour arc, the herbs would have been exposed to sunlight when its strength peaks, to the liminal energy of sunrise and sunset, and to the energy of the full moon.

Remove the jar and cap it. Express your gratitude toward all the energies, spirits, and fairy allies that lent their powers to the water, and give another round of offerings before departing. If you promised any service, make sure that you keep your promise. You can store the water for future use.

If you must harvest any plant materials, whether from parts laying on the ground or clip them from the live plant, consent and offerings are essential. Ask for permission. If you get a no, do take no for an answer, and move on. If permission to harvest is granted, make offerings in the exact same manner as described above: leave something before taking anything, and offer something more after you are done. Show gratitude in every way you can, not only with words but also through deeds. Your service does not have to be anything glamorous: something like picking up the litter that you encounter on a trail is very much appreciated by the local spirits and fairies that may be connected to that place.

If you have prohibitions about using any of the herbs recommended in the charms, spells, and rituals described next, please select different ones based on the information presented in Part 2. I know people whose fairy guides prohibited them to use St. John's Wort, for example. The purpose of this book is to provide readers with enough information for everyone to adapt creatively rather than imitate mindlessly.

To Cleanse a Space from Thick and Heavy Energy:

For a thorough cleanse, I suggest a five-step approach detailed below.

1. **Cleansing with smoke.** Combine mugwort, vervain, and St. John's Wort. You may add frankincense and/or dragon blood. Before proceeding, ask the spirits of the herbs to help you clean the space and make it safe. Ask fairy familiars for assistance. Communicate clearly that you only wish to banish that which is harmful to you and yours and in disharmony with your work and allies. Burn the ingredients on charcoal, and walk through the space you wish to clean. Move clockwise, spiraling from center toward the periphery of the space. As you move around waft the smoke with your hand, fan, or feather, to make it go into all the corners of the room and as much as possible behind and underneath furniture. Insist around windows and door frames. If the herbs in your bowl or censer burn completely before you end cleansing the space, just pause, refill, and continue. Continue cleansing for as long as you feel it is necessary. If you have a favorite charm, incantation, or prayer that is adequate to the situation, chant/recite throughout the cleansing process.

2. **Asperse.** After having finished smoke cleansing, you will asperse the place. In a bowl, preferably copper or ceramic because most fairies are averse to iron, pour water and add either bits of cleansing herbs or a drop or two of the corresponding essential oils. For example, I soak lavender, birch, yarrow, and a few dried elderberry leaves, and use a sprig of rosemary to asperse. Depending on what is available, I might add rosemary to the water as well and use additional twigs of birch and rowan to asperse. If I don't have dried lavender, I use lavender oil instead. As you prepare the aspersing tools, ask each participating

herb to help you clean the space and make it safe. Ask fairy familiars for assistance. Communicate clearly that you only wish to banish that which is harmful to you and yours and in disharmony with your work and allies. State that by the virtue of your will and the powers of the herbs and water, the space is welcoming to your allies and rendered hostile to intruders.

I use rainwater for cleaning spaces. (Read about rainwater in Part 2, Chapter 5.) As I prepare the bowl with water, I speak to the spirit of rain, to the energy encapsulated in the water that I pour and ask it to act like a mightily swelling river that washes out everything that is harmful and negative. I visualize the water sweeping through the space. Or I might think instead of a torrential rain coming down and washing the space. As I visualize, I move around spiraling clockwise, from the center toward the periphery of the space, aspersing as thoroughly as I can. Alternatively, I can use a spray bottle with an adjustable nozzle. If I am concerned about staining walls and furniture, which is something to seriously consider especially when the space I clean is not in my own house, the spray bottle could be a better alternative. When I use the spray, I add the rowan and/or birch – that I would otherwise use as aspersing tools – to the infusion in the bottle.

3. **Warding.** Declare the space is clean, hæl, holy, hallow, or whatever words you prefer to use to describe a state of perfect cleanliness. Affirm that all your allies, familiars, and benevolent beings are welcome into the space. If you are cleansing someone else's house, find out beforehand who are their allies (angels, saints, Aos Sidhe, Álfar, Tuatha Dé Danann, etc.) and welcome those into the space. Ask familiars, allies, spirit guides embodied and disembodied to vigilantly protect the space against any

further intrusion. Place an acorn on each windowsill, tuck a spiky holly leaf, and/or my top favorite – a blackthorn thorn. If you don't have blackthorn you can tuck around some rose thorns or bits of thorny stems. You can use talismans, runes, crystals, mirrors to ramp up protection.

4. **Offerings.** Declare the space safe and perfectly guarded. Express gratitude to all spirits and allies who lent their powers to the process. Present them with food offerings which you will leave around for about 24 hours before discarding. In addition to food you can offer music, poetry, art that you create in their honor, and anything that you believe is a suitable gift for your fairy familiars. (See Part 1, Chapter 3.)

5. **Divination and Omen-taking.** Use the appropriate divination tool (see recommendations in Part 1, Chapter 4) to check in and see if the offerings have been sufficient, well received, and if the space you cleansed is exactly as you wish for it to be. Act accordingly to the input you receive. You may be asked to do another round of cleansing, to offer something specific, or something else along these lines. You might be told that everything is just perfect as it is.

To Hallow a Space in Preparation for Ritual:

Some cleansing is required to prepare a space for ritual, but typically it is not the case to do anything as thorough as the five-step approach mentioned previously. The process should include, however, some form of cleansing and "energizing" by which I mean rendering the space as welcoming as possible for the fairy allies, and less so for the entities you wish to keep out.

Space hallowing should precede any ritual you would conduct (if you usually cast a circle, call quarters, assign guardians, open portals, etc. – you can do so after the space has been hallowed).

If you work indoors, use a broom to lightly sweep through the area. Move from the back of the room toward the front. When finished, drag the broom all the way to the back door of your house and shake it past the threshold: command everything negative to leave the space. A good broom can be made from twigs of birch tied with willow. A bunch of birch twigs is enough. If you don't have such a broom, no worries: any regular broom would do. For increased effect add on the broom's straws a drop of birch oil and rosemary or juniper oil.

If this is an outdoor ritual space, instead of sweeping with the broom you may walk around carrying a staff and pound the ground as you go. The staff can be made of blackthorn, holly, oak, rowan, or ash. (The clean stalk of last year's Christmas tree can be fashioned into a great ritual staff.) I prefer to walk a spiral path, from the center of the space toward the periphery, but you may choose to do it differently. Command everything negative to leave the space.

Asperse or spray an infusion of rose petals, lavender, yarrow, vervain, elecampane, mugwort, and/or St. John's Wort. Use herbs that you feel genuinely connected with and your fairy allies approve of. Use water that is synergistic to the ritual itself. (See Part 2. Chapter 5.)

Burn frankincense to honor the powers you invite to your ritual. If you prefer, you can have frankincense, and any other incense, burning at the time you make offerings.

Continue with the ritual your usual way.

Invite Fairy Blessings over a New Acquisition:

Welcoming into the household new furniture, a new car, appliances, etc. is an important and often overlooked aspect. Second hand items are usually still energetically connected to their previous owner. You wouldn't want to partake from the problems of another, would you? Rarely, but not unheard of, there could be some degree of energetic mismatch between you and the brand new item you just bought; you don't want that either. Blessing newly acquired items is a very old custom, and a useful one too.

To bless a new home, you can perform the same ritual for hallowing a space as described above. Burn frankincense and make offerings to the spirit of the house. If you have a yard, make offerings to the spirits of the land (make sure that you don't leave out anything that is poisonous for wildlife; don't pour spirits straight at the roots of trees and flowers.) Invite your fairy allies to partake. If you have a housewarming party, set aside portions for your fairy familiars and guide, for the fairies and spirits in the house and in your land.

To bless a car, an appliance, or a new piece of furniture, asperse or spray an infusion of rose, lavender, sage, rosemary, vervain – any combination, or one individual herb if you prefer.

I suggest using rainwater to soak the plants (or add the oils to).

You may light some incense, or burn a little mugwort, lavender, and sage (or any cleansing herbs that you favor) wafting the smoke around and if possible inside the object (if you are cleansing and blessing a car or an armoire you would want to open the doors and let the smoke go inside)

Ask your fairy allies to bless the new acquisition, and make offerings as part of the ritual.

Protection

At the risk of repeating myself, I will re-state that protections must be selective. To create protections that act selectively you must know what your fairy allies like, what your enemies dislike or are repelled by, and what are the properties of the ingredients you plan to employ for protection. Protective measures can cover the whole house and property, can be applied to a single room, or to one single person.

Use discernment and have in place alarm systems, report suspicious activity to Police, and if there are threats to your life and safety alert the authorities. Esoteric and energetic protections add one powerful layer but should not be used as a substitute for all the other safety measures.

Whole house and property protection. Start with the house. Do some light energetic cleansing using either smoke or aspersing/spraying. You can burn any of the following herbs, individually or in combination: frankincense, dragon blood, vervain, yarrow, mugwort, St. John's Wort, rosemary. You can use any of these ingredients soaked in the water for spraying or aspersing. Smoke or spray around every space in the house: rooms, bathroom, closets, attic, and basement. State out loud that the space is welcoming for your allies and that all and any intruders are banished. Ask familiars, allies, spirit guides embodied and disembodied to vigilantly protect the space against any kind intrusion. Place an acorn on each windowsill, tuck holly leaves around the windows, and my top favorite – put on each windowsill a blackthorn thorn. If you don't have blackthorn, you can tuck around some rose thorns or a bit of thorny stem. You can place around the house talismans, runes, crystals, mirrors to ramp up protective energy, but discussing these is beyond the scope of this book which focuses on herbs connected to fairies.

Go outside, and walk the boundaries of your land. Whether it is a large backyard, a patio or a small balcony, this is also part of your property and shall be treated with equal care. Smoke or spray using the same ingredients that you used for the house, unless you want to work with something different. Same as you did in the house, state out loud that the space is welcoming for your allies and that all and any intruders are banished. Ask familiars, allies, spirit guides, embodied and disembodied, to vigilantly protect the space against any kind intrusion. You can place thorns under flower pots, stones, or statues. You can grow in your own yard some of the plants known to be protective.

(See Part 2, Chapters 2, 3.) Make offerings to house spirits and fairies, land wights, and to your own allies.

Protect a room. To protect one room only, apply the same set of instructions for protecting the whole house. The steps to follow are the same: cleansing, warding, offerings.

Protect a person. Personal protection involves creating a charm for the person to carry with them, and/or consecrating a piece of jewelry as a protective talisman.

To make a protection pouch, you need a square of cloth from natural fiber or a mix of natural and synthetic. Choose a color that you associate with protection, and in particular with protection granted by your fairy allies. You also need about two feet of cord or ribbon. You have two options. You could gather all the herbs at the center of the square, bring the corners together, tie the square with cord to make a small bundle, and cut all excess material. You can carry the bundle in your pocket, purse, bag etc. Or, from the piece of cloth and the cord, make a small pouch that you can wear around your neck.

Select your herbs. I am only making suggestions, so go carefully through the lists of herbs, trees, and resins and choose what suits you best. I prefer mugwort, elder, blackthorn, St. John's Wort, vervain, yarrow, holly, oak, and jet. Choose at least 3.

First cleanse yourself with smoke: lavender, sage, rosemary, frankincense, one or more of these burned on charcoal, or however you wish. Then pass the pouch/cloth and cord through smoke. Let the smoke reach inside the pouch. Claim the pouch for its purpose: to protect you against all visible and invisible harm. Pick up a tiny amount of each herb, call it by name and ask it to protect you alongside your fairy allies. Then add it to the pouch. After putting in the last herb, add a little bit of your own hair, blow inside the pouch and tie it up with the cord.

Ask your fairy allies to protect you, put on the pouch, make offerings and express your gratitude.

Instead of the protection pouch, or in addition to it, you can consecrate a piece of jewelry as a protective talisman. Choose a pendant, bracelet, earrings – it doesn't matter what it is – as long as it is something that you can wear anytime. What I mean by this is that sumptuous, heavy necklaces with many stones would be great to wear while engaging in magical work but may be difficult to wear at the gym, during a yoga class, hiking etc. Think about what makes practical sense. Cleanse the chosen object by passing it through smoke. You want to remove any previous programming before imprinting your own set of instructions. Use mugwort, rosemary, vervain, and dragon blood, together or separate. As you move the object through smoke, intend for it to release any previous energetic patterns that it holds. Wash with rainwater, or spray just one puff and pass the object quickly through the mist. If water is an absolute no-no, place the object in front of you and visualize heavy rain washing it. Place the object on a flat surface and cover it completely with three or more of the following: mugwort, elder, blackthorn, St. John's Wort, vervain, yarrow, holly, oak, and one or more pieces of jet. Intend for the energy of the herbs to infuse the object and make it into a most potent talisman. Ask your fairy allies to bless it for you. Leave offerings for your fairy guides and Powers that you connect with spiritually, and ask them to oversee the process. Let things sit overnight.

Next day, cleanse yourself with smoke: frankincense alone is enough, but if you choose you may add any herb that you associate with blessings and protection. Pick up the jewelry and put it on. Give thanks to the spirit of the plants you used, the fairies and the Powers overseeing the process. You may use the same herbs to energize another object. Rely on your own intuition to get a sense whether the herbs still hold enough energy or are exhausted. When you must dispose of the herbs, do so respectfully by composting them or discarding them outside by a tree or in a flowerbed. Do not treat the herbs as trash. If you used jet and crystals, you can surely keep them for further use.

To Bring Harmony at Work and at Home

Make offerings to the spirits of the place on a regular basis. Set up a little space for them. It can be a tiny corner on your desk, on a shelf, or on the fireplace mantle. Place a small bowl with rose petals, or make a potpourri of colorful petals and pleasant smelling herbs such as rosemary and sage. If you work in an office where co-workers come and go, you can keep a small saucer and a coffee cup near the floral arrangement. Apple slices, grapes, crackers, homemade cookies, water, juice, and coffee (because, why not?) can be offered without drawing unwanted attention.

To Attract Love

Start by making an offering to your fairy allies. Then communicate your intent and ask for assistance.

Make a small cloth pouch, or buy one. It should be something that you can wear the same way you would carry a pendant on a necklace or cord. The color of cloth shall be something that you personally connect with love and attraction. Go beyond the pink or red stereotypes unless, of course, these are colors that you associate with love and attraction.

Take a bath. Add to the bathwater a drop or two of rose oil, amber oil, and any other flower or herb that you associate with love and magic. Read beforehand about the herbs you wish to use. While soaking in the herb-infused bathwater, meditate on the herb's properties. Feel their energy mingling with your own. After the bath, get the pouch and pass it through smoke. Burn lavender, sage, or a combination of both.

The ingredients for the pouch are: a bit of apple peel, rose petals, a piece of ivy stem, leaf or both, a drop of honey, and a tiny bit of your hair. Pick up each herb and while holding ask it to bring its qualities to the pouch: rose for attractiveness, apple for youthfulness and vitality, ivy for fast growing and tying everything together in a long lasting bond. Add honey for sweetness and to invite the energy of cooperation, common goals, and fruitful partnership. Add a bit of hair, blow into the pouch, and close it tight. Hold the charm between your hands and feel all the energies in it becoming part of your own. Wear the pouch or carry it with you in a pocket or purse.

It is counterproductive to think of one specific person attempting to bind them to you against their feelings. It doesn't end well. The charm is meant to attract that which is most resonant with you and most rewarding in the long run.

For General Wellbeing

Gather first the following ingredients:

- Oak, a tiny piece of bark and/or 2-3 acorns
- Yarrow, about a spoon of dried flowers
- A few rose petals or a drop or two of rose water or oil
- Birch, few catkins, bits of twigs, leaves, or birch oil
- Willow, leaves, a tiny piece of bark, or twig
- Elder, few berries or flowers, or few drops of elderberry syrup found in health stores
- Amber, one piece or few drops of amber oil
- Apple, dried bits of apple or apple peel

From a piece of white cloth make a satchel, or simply gather the ingredients at the center of the cloth and pick up the corners to make a bundle that you tie up with cord. Make offerings to your fairy allies and prepare for meditation. Hold onto the satchel while doing the mediation from Part 1. When see fairy guide(s) ask for help and support toward your own health and wellbeing. Surrender to the process.

You might do the meditation sitting in the tub, in which case you can have the loose herbs in the water or soak the satchel in the tub with you.

To Improve Communication with Fairy Beings

To attract fairy presence and improve communication with fairy allies, there are several herbs which could be of assistance. There are multiple ways to invite the help of these plant allies. One way is growing hollyhocks, mugwort, roses, foxglove bushes, lavender, elecampane, cowslip, or violets in your yard, patio, balcony, etc.

Looking through a loop made of an ash twig at specific times (Midsummer, Bealtaine/ Walpurgisnacht/ May Eve. Winter Solstice, etc.) could facilitate seeing fairies. Sleeping inside a fairy ring that grows under a female oak tree on a Friday night is also supposed to help seeing fairies. (Review the entries for Ash and Oak in Part 2, Chapter 2.)

You can craft an amulet to facilitate connection and communication with fairies. Make or purchase a small pouch that you can wear on a cord around the neck. Whether you make it or buy it, choose a color that you associate with fairies. I am suggesting a number of herbs and materials to consider. Chose three or more among these and don't hesitate to add others that you know from personal gnosis:

- Rose petals, or oil
- Lavender, dried herb or oil
- Elecampane
- Lady's bedstraw
- Primrose
- Vervain
- Violets
- Holly, leaf and/or berry

- Hawthorn berries,
- Blackthorn, leaf, flower, thorn, bit of bark
- Ash, leaf, bit of wood or bark
- Apple, flower or a bit of the fruit
- Four leaf clover or wood sorrel
- Mugwort
- Amber, solid or a drop of amber oil

Place on the altar the selected herbs, the empty pouch, water from a place that you connect with fairies (snow water, rain water, or any holy water that you made), honey, and offerings to fairy allies and to the kind of fairies that you seek to connect with (Ljosalfar, Svartalfar, Aos Sidhe, Rusalii, Sânziene, Vila, Rusalki, etc.). It is important to know the lore surrounding these beings, because you would want to really know their preferences, likes and dislikes. Do your best to make the offerings personalized rather than generic. Meditate briefly. Invite the fairies that you seek to connect with to bless the items for the charm and enjoy the offerings. It is best if you can do this at sunset, leave everything sit overnight, and complete the ritual the next day at sunrise, noon, or sunset.

After having left the offerings and all materials on the altar for a reasonable amount of time, light up frankincense and cleanse yourself with smoke. Pass the pouch through the smoke. Pick up the herbs one at a time: invoke its qualities and ask it to facilitate your sight and connection with fairies. Give thanks to the herb before putting it in the pouch. One by one, gather inside the pouch all the herbs that you chose. Now add one droplet of honey: intend for the relationship with fairy allies to be one of cooperation and be fruitful for everyone involved. Add one drop of water: intend for your gift of seeing and communicating to grow strong, and for your relationship with the respective fairy beings to grow strong and healthy. Close the pouch and put it on. Wear the pouch for the next 24 hours to see how it feels. Place it under your pillow at night and monitor your dreams because dreams are one of the channels that fairy allies use to communicate. Wear the pouch during rituals, while visiting places which are connected to fairies, or whenever your intuition tells you that wearing it is a good idea.

Conclusion

I hope that you enjoyed reading this book and you found it a useful resource. I hope the material presented here will help you hone your skills and strengthen your connection with fairies. My goal has been to make fairy-powered herbalism accessible to everyone, to open the path for those who are new to fairy magic, and hopefully, to provide seasoned practitioners with a neatly organized compendium of fairy herbs for fairy magic.

For the new practitioners, I shared from my own approach to magic that involves fairy herbs because I believe in the usefulness of templates to follow, especially for things that you never tried before. It is good to have a map when venturing in uncharted territory, but also it's important to bear in mind that at some point someone had to go first into uncharted territory to draw the first map. Learn the lore, but make space for exploration. I wish for the material presented here, especially the charms and rituals in Part 3 to ignite curiosity and desire to try new things and make new saplings grow from old roots.

All old and classical knowledge, whether witchcraft or quantum mechanics was at some point brand new, and some among the greatest discoveries began as accidents. I believe it is important that we study the old lore, and dedicate time to understand fairies within their native cultural context. We can thus build on knowledge that stood the test of time and in moving on to find our own ways we create materials for the next generations and invite them to do the same. Fairy witchcraft is not a relic but a living aspect of the present. Because fairy spirituality is a continuum, knowledge of past traditions influences the way we approach the fairy path today; what we do today will at some point influence the fairy path for those walking it tomorrow. It is a big responsibility.

Endnotes

1.   For the sake of simplicity and clarity, throughout this book the word fairy is used as an umbrella term which covers the Irish sidhe, Norse Álfar, Anglo-Saxon alfs, Romanian zâne, and all beings that are described as otherworldly, humanoid, non-monstrous, with magical powers. Related to the Álfar, the names elf and elves should not be confused with the commercialized versions, Santa's elves.

2.   I published another two books. *Where Fairies Meet: Parallels between Irish and Romanian Fairy Traditions* is the first ever published side-by-side analysis of fairy traditions of Ireland and Romania. *A Fairy Path: The Memoir of a Young Fairy Seer in Training'* is an autobiographical work detailing the author's childhood in Romania, and the apprenticeship with her Grandmother, a respected medicine woman and fairy seer. Also part of my work is the blog, Whispers in the Twilight intended as a free resource for everyone with an interest in fairy-based spirituality. Last but not least, I teach a 3-part course, *Fairycrafting: The Art of Fairy Magic*, which focuses on the practical aspects of building relationships and working in partnership with fairy allies.

3.   Theosophy is a philosophical and spiritual movement which began in the nineteenth century. It drew from Gnosticism, Neoplatonism, Rosicrucianism, and Alchemy, especially the fifteenth century work of Paracelsus. From this mix of ideas which blend with the Romanticism of the Victorian era, the trend of infantilized, diminutive fairies corresponding to elements and functioning as nature spirits emerged.

4.   The Schools Collection is the result of the Irish government's effort to preserve the native lore, folklore, and traditions.

The project was launched in the 1930s. Over a period of a few years, school children were assigned the task of collecting stories from around their communities. Collected first as they were handed in by children – handwritten notes – the documents have been transferred on microfilm, and currently are in the process of being transcribed and digitized. The School Collection's Archive is a priceless resource and can be visited at https://www.duchas.ie/en/cbes

5.   Bessie Dunlop was charged for witchcraft, arrested, interrogated, tortured, tried, sentenced, and executed in 1576, Edinburg. Details about her trial and confessions are available at https://en.wikipedia.org/wiki/Bessie_Dunlop_of_Lynn and https://www.nationalarchives.gov.uk/education/resources/early-modern-witch-trials/church-role-in-accusations/ . In her book *Cunning-Folk and Familiar Spirits*, Emma Wilby analyzes in great detail Bessie's declarations about her fairy familiar, Tom Reid.

6.   For in depth information on how to work with fairies and how to approach modern fairy witchcraft, consult the resources listed in Appendix B. *Fairy Witchcraft'* by Morgan Daimler is a perfect place to start. Gods, Elves & Witches by Cat Heath is a complex resource for those interested in Elves, as they appear in Norse, Germanic, and Anglo-Saxon traditions. Similarly, *Elves, Wights, and Trolls'* by Kveldulf Gundarsson is useful for those interested in partnerships with Norse fairy beings. I personally like the exercises suggested in *Faery Craft'* by Emily Carding, also listed in Appendix B.

7.   You can watch Ivanka getting into trance and listen to the interview on YouTube: "Dr. Maria Vivod, The Fairy Seers of Eastern Serbia" https://www.youtube.com/watch?v=ekXf7Z8G21o

8. The Psalms of King Solomon mention frankincense and calamus (dragon blood) as precious gifts in a category with gold. See Song of Solomon 3:6; 4:13-14.

9. Derived from Old Norse hæl and Proto-Germanic hanhilaz. It means generous, bountiful, kind, liberal.

10. There are other plants known by the name of lady's fingers. One is a species of cactus, *Mammillaria*, growing in Mexico. Another plant is okra or bindhi, *Abelmoscus esculentus*, which grows in India and parts of the Middle East. Yet another plant that goes by the name of lady fingers is an orchid, *Caladenia*, that only grows in Australia. None of these plants were growing in Ireland in the nineteenth century. Thus, it isn't likely for Biddy Early to have used such exotic ingredients or recommend them to people in her village.

11. Greek fairy-beings portrayed as beautiful women, connected to woods and vegetation.

Appendix A

Fairy Gardens

Fairy gardens may conjure the image of colorful flower beds, artificial little ponds, statuary of winged humanoids, and fairy houses tied on to trees or hiding between bushes. While this is what fairy gardens are for some, it is not at all what I have in mind. In the context of this book and in line with the material presented here, by fairy garden I mean an outdoor or indoor sanctuary dedicated to fairy allies where plants they have an affinity for play an important part.

You might as well leave a patch of garden undisturbed for the land spirits and fairy denizens to use it as they please. However, this is not always possible. Many people like myself live in neighborhoods where homeowner associates issue fines for "neglected" backyards. A fairy garden can occupy relatively little space, big just enough to accommodate what you believe is essential, and provide a little nice space for offerings. It may be large enough for you to have a spot where to sit and meditate when you seek to connect to fairy allies. It may be so large that you could hold rituals inside. Or your fairy garden may fit in a planter.

In your fairy garden, you can have rocks, statues, lights or lanterns that you could light up on occasion, and, of course, plants. If you have no outdoor space and the idea of building a fairy garden appeals to you, use a planter that you can fit on the porch, patio, balcony, or windowsill. Even if your fairies are the average human size or taller, do not worry about them fitting in a miniature garden. This is devotional work more than anything else, and following the consecration ritual, fairies will connect with you through the garden that you have made for them. Fairies can assume any size and any shape they wish, so don't be concerned that the rock you placed among the flowers in the planter is too small for them to sit on. More importantly, time and space are distorted when interacting with the Otherworld and its inhabitants. In another dimension, on the Fairy side, the tiny garden that fits on your windowsill can expand to the size of a park.

What you plant depends not so much on your own personal taste, but it is mainly related to what your fairy allies prefer. Read Part 2 carefully to find out what plant appeals to what type of fairy beings and optimize the environment for the fairy alliances you seek to build. Sometimes the information appears to be contradictory. For such cases I will paraphrase Cat Heath in saying that as a rule of thumb, hæl and holy herbs do not antagonize hæl and holy beings. (I don't mean holy in the Christian sense.) For more suggestions about what to plant in a magical garden, I recommend reading the chapter Magical Gardening from *Kitchen Witchcraft* by Rachel Patterson. The book is listed in the Appendix C, Recommended Readings and Resources.

In the end, your garden may have lots of pastel flowers and even glitter if this is what your fairy allies like and recommend, or it may be all briar and blackthorn, or roses, or elecampane smiling in the sun.

I will use my own outdoor fairy space as an example. A relatively long time ago fairies claimed a certain tree in the backyard, an elm more precisely. This should not be so surprising since in Norse tradition elm is also called elven. (Case in point, fairies will ultimately lead you to what they want in their garden even when you think it is your garden.) I wasn't planning on creating any kind of dedicated outdoor fairy space, but over time I ended up building at the base of the tree a small mound, with few stones on top fashioned like a portal tomb, or dolmen. There are two other stones by the mound, a white obelisk-like one on which I pour the liquid offerings, and a white, triangular, flat stone on which I leave food offerings during ritual. I interfere minimally with this setting that grew organically from my fairy path, as it meandered over these years. I am happy with whatever vegetation grows around, which is mostly mushrooms. I have space to sit there and meditate, contemplate, brainstorm, and talk to my fairy allies. I would like to plant a few things around, but first I shall consult my own guides. As the saying goes, if it isn't broken don't fix it and I wouldn't want to do anything to upset the existing balance.

Appendix B

Honoring Fairies on Special Occasions
(Adaptation from an old Romanian ritual)

I was very young when I first learned from my grandmother about the tradition of making offerings to fairies. I am presenting here the ritual as my grandmother remembered it from the times she was a child followed by the adapted version in which I participated.

In certain parts of Romania, the ritual was performed on the Wednesday before Easter. In the evening, a fire was made outdoors with three kinds of wood: field maple *(Acer campestre)*, hazel *(Corylus avelana)*, and dogwood *(Cornus florida)*. A white tablecloth was laid on the ground, and on it there was a dish with water for fairies to refresh themselves upon arrival, three cups with fresh drinking water, and three small loaves of bread. Frankincense and myrrh were thrown in the fire to purify the surroundings, as the fragrance spread around. People would stay around until the fire was out and then retire for the night leaving out the offerings for fairies.

When Grandma taught me this ritual, we lacked the possibility to light a bonfire with the required woods. We set up the offerings for the fairies in the gazebo in the backyard. We covered the table with a white tablecloth, and at the center of the table we gathered a few candles in jars. We lit up the candles and placed them around the dish with water for fairies to wash their hands and faces, three cups with fresh drinking water, and three small loaves of bread. We sat chairs around the table, burned frankincense, and waited for the candles to go out. Then Grandma and I went inside, leaving the offerings on the table.

I no longer do the ritual in conjunction with Easter Sunday, but I still like to do it on other occasions such as Spring and Fall Equinoxes or on May Day Eve. Sometimes I feel drawn to do the ritual as close in its form as I learned it but other times I change things such as adding more items beside the bread offerings, putting rose petals in the water for washing, singing, playing music, reciting something, etc.

Appendix C

Recommended Reading and Resources

Books

Carding, Emily, *Faery Craft. Weaving Connections with the Enchanted Realm*, 2020

Daimler, Morgan, *Fairy Witchcraft. A Neopagan's Guide to the Celtic Fairy Faith*, 2014

Daimler, Morgan, *A Guide to the Celtic Fairies*, 2017

Heath, Cat *Elves, Witches & Gods: Spinning Old Heathen Magic in the Modern Day*, 2021

Heath, Cat, *Essays from the Crossroads*, 2016

Lenihan, Edmund, *In Search of Biddy Early*, 1987

Patterson, Rachel, *Pagan Portals – Kitchen Witchcraft: Crafts of a Kitchen Witch*, 2013

Sigmundsdottir, Alda, *The Little Book of the Hidden People*, 2021

Simina, Daniela, *Where Fairies Meet: Parallels Between Irish and Romanian Fairy Traditions*, 2023

Simina, Daniela, *A Fairy Path: The Memoir of a Young Fairy Seer in Training*, 2023

Wilby, Emma, *Cunning-Folk and Familiar Spirits: Shamanistic Visionary Traditions in Early Modern British Witchcraft and Magic*, 2006

Young, Simon, *Ann Jefferies and the Fairies: A Source Book for a Seventeenth-Century Cornish Fairy Witch*, 2021

Blogs and Media Channels

Blythe Rhymer, "The Raven and the Lotus", http://theravenandthelotus.com

Seo Helrune, "Seo Helrune: Elves and Witchcraft, Seidr and Grimoires" https://seohelrune.com

Morgan Daimler, "Living Liminally", https://lairbhan. blogspot.com

Morgan Daimler, "Fairies" https://www.youtube.com/ playlist?list=PLgPP3Ew0XJBKk5Nh5icavd_hmMnXfcYrA

Alexandra Nic Bhé Chuille, "Bhe Chuille and Dinand: My Understanding of Two Obscure Irish Goddesses", https:// www.7serendipities.com/blog/be-chuille-and-dinand

Daniela Svartðheidrin Simina, "Whispers in the Twilight", https://whispersinthetwilight.blogspot.com/2021/08/

Daniela Svartðheidrin Simina, https://www.youtube.com/ @danielasimina

Classes

Daimler, Morgan, "Pulling the Wings off Fairies", available through the Irish Pagan School https://irishpaganschool.com

Daimler, Morgan, "The Fairy Faith in Practice", available through the Irish Pagan School https://irishpaganschool.com

Heath, Cat, "Elves and Witches: A Survival Guide" To access the class materials contact Cat Heath at seo.helrune@gmail.com

Heath, Cat, "Charms, Wihta, and Story: An Animistic Approach to Modern Heathen Magic" Parts 1 and 2. To access the class materials contact Cat Heath at seo.helrune@gmail.com

Bibliography

Beckett, J., (2015) 4 Steps to Re-Enchant the World, https://www.patheos.com/blogs/johnbeckett/2015/09/4-steps-to-re-enchant-the-world.html last visited Jan 6, 2023

Creangā, I., (2008) *Povesti*

Cunningham, S., (1985) *Cunningham's Encyclopedia of Magical Herbs*

Dafni, A., (2019) Myrtle, Basil, Rosemary, and Three-Lobed Sage as Ritual Plants in the Monotheistic Religions: an Historical-Ethnobotanical Comparison, https://botanica.ugr.es/pages/publicaciones/separatas/2019_Econ_Bot/%21 accessed January 31, 2023

Daimler, M., (2020) *Living Fairy*

_____ (2016) *Fairycraft: Following the Path of Fairy Witchcraft*

_____ (2011) Familiars and why I don't believe in them, retrieved at https://lairbhan.blogspot.com/2011/08/familiars-and-why-i-I-believe-in.html , last accessed January 6, 2023

_____ (2014) The Witch, the Bean Feasa, and the Fairy Doctor in Irish Culture, retrieved at https://www.academia.edu/17823067/The_Witch_the_Bean_Feasa_and_the_Fairy_Doctor_in_Irish_Culture last accessed January 8, 2023

_____ (2020) *A New Dictionary of Fairies: A 21st Century Exploration of Celtic and Related Western European Fairies*

_____ (2022) *Aos Sidhe*

_____ (2023) *Freya*

Eachtra Condla, Lebor Na hUidre, retrieved in Mary Jones' Celtic Literature Collective at https://www.maryjones.us/ctexts/connla.html last accessed on 01/05/2023

Eliade, M., (1973) Notes on Cālusari

Gantz, J., (1982) *Early Myths and Sagas*

Ghinoiu, I., (2020) *Romanian Folk Almanac*

Gundarsson, K., (1993) *Teutonic Magic. Folk Beliefs and Practices of the Northern Tradition*

_____ (2007) *Elves, Wights, and Trolls*

Halpin, D., (2019), Folklore, Fairies, and the Pear Tree, retrieved at https://www.facebook.com/CircleStoriesDavidHalpin/posts/folklore-fairies-and-the-pear-treealthough-the-pear-tree-is-not-believed-to-be-n/878217762526901/ last accessed January 27, 2023

Heath, C., (2021) *Elves, Witches & Gods: Spinning Old Heathen Magic in the Modern Day*

_____ (2022) *Elves and Witches: A Survival Guide*

_____ (2022) *Mound Magic*

Hopman Evert, E., (2010) *Scottish Herbs and Fairy Lore*

Ispirescu, P., (2016) *Romanian Folk Tales*

Jacobs, J., (1894) The Faith of the Children of Lir, https://www.luminarium.org/mythology/ireland/cormacfairy.htm last visited January 14, 2023

Jones's Celtic Encyclopedia, https://www.maryjones.us/jce/dagda.html) last visited January 26, 2023

Kligman, G., (1981) *Călus. Symbolic Transformation in Romanian Ritual*

Lenihan, E., (1987) *In Search of Biddy Early*

_____ (2004) *Meeting the Other Crowd: The Fairy Stories of Hidden Ireland*

Mac Coitir, N., (2015) *Ireland's Wild Plants*

_____ (2018) *Ireland's Trees*

O'Brien, L., (2021), *Fairy Faith in Ireland*

O Crualaoich, G., (2003) The Book of The Cailleach. Magic and Religious Cures (2014) Ask About Ireland. Retrieved from http://askaboutireland.ie/reading-roomJhistory-heritage/folklore-of-ireland/folklore-in-ireland/healers-and-healing/magic-and-religious-cures/

Paxon, D., (2021) *Taking Up the Runes: A Complete Guide to Using Runes in Spells, Rituals, Divination, and Magic*

Pócs, E., (1989), *Fairies and Witches at the Boundary of South-Eastern and Central Europe*

Seo Helrune, (2018) *Restoration, Not Re-enchantment*

Sigmundsdottir, A., (2021) *The Little Book of the Hidden People*

Simina, D., (2023) *Where Fairies Meet: Parallels Between Irish and Romanian Fairy Traditions*

_____ (2023) *A Fairy Path. The Memoir of a Young Fairy Seer in Training*

_____ (2022) Reclamation of Fairy Folklore and Traditions in Post-Communist Romania, https://www.academia.edu/86817044/Reclamation_of_Fairy_Folklore_and_Traditions_in_Post_Comunist_Romania

Starling, M., (2022) *Welsh Witchcraft. A Guide to the Spirits, Lore, and Magic of Wales*

Starza, L., (2023) *Rounding the Wheel of the Year*

Story Archaeology, (2014) Echtrae Tadgh Mac Céin, https://storyarchaeology.com/rowing-around-immrama-7-echtrae-tadhg-mac-cein-the-adventures-of-tadhg-son-of-cian/ last accessed January 13, 2023

Sturluson, S., (1990) *Heimskringla, or the Lives of the Norse Kings*

Sturluson, S., (1995) *Prose Edda*

Unknown, Cath Maige Tuired, CELT The Corpus of Electronic Text, https://celt.ucc.ie/published/T300010/index.html last accessed January 13, 2023

Vivod, M., (2014) *Radmila – The Fairy Clairvoyant. Rethinking Ethnopsychiatry – A Case Study From Serbia*

_____ (2018) *The Fairy Seers from Eastern Serbia: Seeing Fairies – Speaking through Trance*

Wilby, E., (2006) Cunning-Folk and Familiar Spirits: Shamanistic Visionary Traditions in Early Modern British Witchcraft and Magic

Wilde, L., (1991) *Irish Cures, Mystic Charms & Superstition*

Young, S., (2021

About the Author

Daniela Simina grew up in Romania, immersed in the rich local fairy lore. When young, she apprenticed with her grandmother, a fairy seer and medicine woman, and became a medicine woman and fairy witch herself.

Daniela is passionate about researching Irish, Romanian, and Norse-Germanic fairy folklore and traditions. She studied under the guidance of scholars and writers invested in preserving the historical and folkloric heritage. Daniela Simina travels periodically to Ireland, to cultivate the connection with the Fair Folk in situ. In addition to writing, she teaches classes on energy healing, various esoteric subjects, and of course, fairies.

From the Author

Thank you for purchasing *Fairy Herbs for Fairy Magic: A Practical Guide to Fairy Herbalism*. My sincere hope is that you derived as much from reading this book as I have in creating it. If you have a few moments, please feel free to add your review of the book to your favorite online site for feedback. Also, if you would like to connect with other books that I have coming in the near future, please visit my Facebook author pages for news on upcoming works, recent blog posts and events:

https://www.facebook.com/DanielaSiminaAuthorPage
https://whispersinthetwilight.blogspot.com

Sincerely, Daniela Simina

You may also like

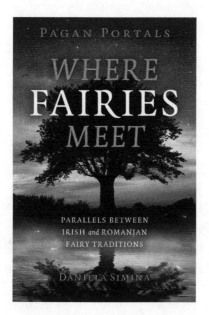

Where Fairies Meet

by Daniela Simina

Parallels between Irish and Romanian Fairy Traditions

978-1-80341-019-7 (Paperback)
978-1-80341-230-6 (e-book)

Bestsellers from Moon Books

Pagan Portals Series

The Morrigan
Meeting the Great Queens
Morgan Daimler
Ancient and enigmatic, the Morrigan reaches out to us.
On shadowed wings and in raven's call, meet the ancient Irish
goddess of war, battle, prophecy, death, sovereignty, and magic.
Paperback: 978-1-78279-833-0 ebook: 978-1-78279-834-7

The Awen Alone
Walking the Path of the Solitary Druid
Joanna van der Hoeven
An introductory guide for the solitary Druid, The Awen Alone will
accompany you as you explore, and seek out your own place within
the natural world.
Paperback: 978-1-78279-547-6 ebook: 978-1-78279-546-9

Moon Magic
Rachel Patterson
An introduction to working with the phases of the Moon, what they
are and how to live in harmony with the lunar year and to utilise all
the magical powers it provides.
Paperback: 978-1-78279-281-9 ebook: 978-1-78279-282-6

Hekate
A Devotional
Vivienne Moss
Hekate, Queen of Witches and the Shadow-Lands, haunts the pages
of this devotional bringing magic and enchantment into your lives.
Paperback: 978-1-78535-161-7 ebook: 978-1-78535-162-4

Readers of ebooks can buy or view any of these bestsellers by clicking on the live link in the title. Most titles are published in paperback and as an ebook. Paperbacks are available in traditional bookshops. Both print and ebook formats are available online.

Find more titles and sign up to our readers' newsletter
www.collectiveinkbooks.com/paganism

For video content, author interviews and more, please subscribe to our YouTube channel.

MoonBooksPublishing

Follow us on social media for book news, promotions and more:

Facebook: Moon Books

Instagram: @MoonBooksCI

X: @MoonBooksCI

TikTok: @MoonBooksCI